CHARLES

Christopher W. Daniels
Culford School, Suffolk
Sometime Schoolmaster Fellow Commoner
Sidney Sussex College, Cambridge

and

John Morrill
Fellow and Senior Tutor
Selwyn College, Cambridge

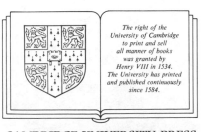

The right of the
University of Cambridge
to print and sell
all manner of books
was granted by
Henry VIII in 1534.
The University has printed
and published continuously
since 1584.

CAMBRIDGE UNIVERSITY PRESS

Cambridge
New York   New Rochelle
Melbourne   Sydney

Published by the Press Syndicate of the University of Cambridge
The Pitt Building, Trumpington Street, Cambridge CB2 1RP
32 East 57th Street, New York, NY 10022, USA
10 Stamford Road, Oakleigh, Melbourne 3166, Australia

First published 1988

Printed in Great Britain at the University Press, Cambridge

British Library cataloguing in publication data
Daniels, Christopher W.
   Charles I.
   1. Charles, I, *King of England*   2. Great
   Britain – Kings and rulers – Biography
   I. Title   II. Morrill, John
   942.06′2′0924   DA396.A2

Library of Congress cataloging in publication data

Daniels, Christopher W.
   Charles I.

   Bibliography: p. 118
   1. Charles I, King of England, 1600–1649.
2. Great Britain – History – Charles I, 1625–1649.
3. Great Britain – Kings and rulers – Biography.
I. Morrill, J. S. (John Stephen)   II. Title.
DA396.A2D36   1988   941.06′2′0924 [B]   87-24979

ISBN 0 521 31728 2

Contents

To R. W. Wilkinson and R. N. Dore –
inspiring teachers

Acknowledgements

The division of labour of this book is complicated: both authors take responsibility for the overall shape and contents. CWD is principally responsible for Chapters 3 and 5, JSM for Chapters 1, 2 and 6. The remaining chapters are amalgams of ideas. In the course of planning the book, the authors received very considerable stimulus and help from a number of friends and colleagues, including Richard Cust, Peter Donald, Anthony Milton, Conrad Russell, and especially David Smith and Kevin Sharpe. The authors are also grateful for the advice, encouragement and professionalism of the Desk Editor at the Press, Stephanie Boyd, and her predecessor, Sally Taylor.

The authors and publisher are grateful to the following for permission to reproduce illustrations and extracts:

p. 5 C. Carlton, *Charles I*, Routlege and Kegan Paul; pp. 5–6 K. Sharpe, 'Crown, Parliament and the Localities' in *English Historical Review*, 1986; p. 6 K. Sharpe, 'The Personal Rule of Charles I' in *Before the English Civil War 1603–42*, ed. H. Tomlinson, 1983; 3.11 R. Strong, *Charles I on Horseback*, 1972, reproduced by permission of Penguin Books Ltd; 3.17 K. Sharpe, 'Crown and Parliament', ed. L. M. Smith, *The Making of Britain: The Age of Expansion*, 1986, Macmillan; 7.2 C. Carlton, in J. G. A. Pocock (ed.), *Three British Revolutions, 1641, 1688, 1776*, 1981, Folger Shakespeare Library; 7.4 L. Stone, *Causes of the English Revolution*, 1972, Routlege and Kegan Paul; 7.6 C. Russell, 'Why did Charles I fight the Civil War?', *History Today*, June 1984.
Illustrations: 3.1 Reproduced by gracious permission of Her Majesty The Queen; 3.2 The Mansell Collection; 3.3 Reproduced by courtesy of the Trustees, The National Gallery, London; 3.4 Courtauld Institute of Art; 3.5, 3.6 and 3.7 Crown copyright, reproduced with the permission of the Controller of Her Majesty's Stationery Office; 3.9 and 3.10 Devonshire Collection, Chatsworth. Reproduced by permission of The Chatsworth Settlement Trustees and the Courtauld Institute of Art; 3.15 a and b, 3.16 a and b The Fitzwilliam Museum, Cambridge.

Cover illustration Three Heads of Charles I by Van Dyck; reproduced by gracious permission of Her Majesty The Queen

Preface

This book is designed for use alongside other works. It is not intended to offer a comprehensive background to the events of 1625–42, still less to explain the origins of the English civil war. Assuming that in a personal monarchy the personality, policy preferences and public actions of the monarch play a major part in the shaping of events, the book concentrates on King Charles I. It looks at his actions and at how they were perceived by his contemporaries. Before using the book, students should gain some sense of the course of events between 1625 and 1642, such as can be gained from any of the items in the Bibliography (see page 118). The book is planned for group discussion or for written exercises, and the questions are simply indications of what we think are appropriate. Teachers and students might like to design their own questions. If the practice of using primary-source materials in the classroom is to develop *historical* skills, then it must not become a set of mechanical exercises. There is only one question a historian should ask of any primary source: 'What does this contribute to our understanding of this period of history?'. That question necessarily involves us in putting a document into context – what do we know of its provenance, bias, honesty? What does it tell us that is confirmed by other evidence, and what in it cannot be confirmed? How far does the document confirm other sources, how far does it contradict other sources, and how can we decide which is reliable? The questions we have set are designed to help students to read documents carefully, and to relate them to other evidence. Some documents may require students to refer to other books in order to be able to make sense of or to evaluate the extracts, but we have tried to ensure that nothing is demanded that cannot be found in a reasonable school or college library.

Introduction

Between 1327 and 1485, reigning monarchs were deposed on no fewer than seven occasions (1327, 1399, 1461, 1470, 1471, 1483, 1485). But on each of those occasions a rival claimant took over, and the institution of monarchy itself was not questioned. Although wars over the succession were an ever-present threat throughout the sixteenth century, that threat receded once the Stuarts were on the throne. Charles I's accession in 1625 was probably the most untroubled since that of Henry V in 1413 (and certainly since the accession of Henry VIII in 1509). Yet after seventeen years on the throne, Charles found himself involved in a civil war that split the nation in two. Seven years later he was not only (like those predecessors) deposed, he was unprecedently put on trial, convicted of treason against his people, and publicly executed; and monarchy itself was abolished. Clearly Charles I was not one of England's more successful kings! But historians have never ceased to debate how far he was the author of his own destruction. Was the scourge of civil war and the trauma of regicide a judgement on Charles, or on a system of government over which he haplessly presided? Did he inherit and blunder away a strong position? Or did he inherit an untenable position? Was he a king who sought and failed to change the nature of monarchical authority in Britain? Or was he a king who sought to stem the aggressive demands of powerful groups in society, who wished to change the system of government so as to increase their own authority at the expense of the personal power of the Crown?

Such questions need to be approached from a number of angles. It is important to consider, for example, the resources at the Crown's disposal, and the extent of the Crown's dependence upon several social groups whose wealth and standing had changed over time. It is important to understand how far there was agreement or disagreement about the nature of the Constitution; and the limits which that Constitution imposed on the Crown, legal system, and representatives of the Estates of the Realm gathered in Parliament. But any such enquiry must have, as a central focus, the personality and policies of the King. Between 1625 and 1641 Charles I could and did choose all his own ministers and advisers; he could and did select his own bishops and archbishops, and all the judges; and he could and did choose his own foreign and domestic policies. To say that there were practical constraints on him (lack of money, lack of military force etc.) is not helpful. The only constraints that matter are those recognized by Charles himself, not those recognized by historians. To do that which was foolish (even that which was politically suicidal) was one of his choices. Even if impersonal social and economic forces were shaping the destiny of the nation, the precise nature of the crisis of government in the 1640s must owe a great deal to the King himself. Had Charles I been a Puritan fanatic, for example, the events of these years would obviously have taken a radically different course. (This is not to claim that twentieth-century Britain would have been different; and it is not to say that there would not have been a civil war in the seventeenth century. But it is to say that England would not have had that type of civil war when it did, in or after 1642.)

This introduction – and the book as a whole – cannot help but shape your conclusions. We have had to select barely 100 extracts from literally tens of thousands of available documents bearing on Charles' reign. We have had to divide the subject into six main areas, and that imposes a shape on the reign which is *our* construction. Remember that this book – like all collections of sources – is no more 'objective' than any history book. We can assure you, however, that our main purpose has been, as far as possible, to open questions, not to assume answers. But the selection of certain questions necessarily suppresses others, and highlights certain features of the reign at the expense of others. Some historians will think that we have selected material which stresses conflict and disagreement rather than material which demonstrates the continuing coincidence of interest between Crown and people, and more specifically Crown and gentry-élites. Some people in England were – as you will see – afraid of the growth of tyranny, of overmighty rulers; but they were also afraid of anarchy, of the collapse of the government and reversion to the lawlessness of the fifteenth century, or of much of western Europe in the sixteenth century. Similarly, almost everyone down to 1642 wanted a State Church to which everyone must belong, although they might disagree about the structure and practice of that State Church.

The first six chapters seem to divide up Charles' life as straightforwardly and manageably as possible. In Chapter 1 there are some glimpses of Charles' childhood and early manhood up to his accession to the throne in 1625. Then there are some indications, in Chapter 2, of the problems of his early years, up to the dissolution of the third Parliament in 1629 and the beginning of what is most usually known as the 'Personal Rule' – the eleven years from 1629 to 1640 during which he chose not to call a Parliament. That Personal Rule is considered in three parallel chapters: Chapter 3 is intended to reveal Charles' aspirations through his artistic patronage; Chapter 4 examines his religious policies; and Chapter 5 looks at his government of the State. (This chapter also reminds us that he was

King of Scotland and Ireland, as well as of England, and that the collapse of this authority in the latter followed its collapse in first Scotland and then Ireland.) The sixth chapter looks at the events of 1640–2 and at Charles' part in deciding to break the political deadlock by a recourse to arms.

In order to help you to make best use of these documents, we offer here a limited introduction to Charles' personality and policies. We are isolating three characteristics about which we think there is a scholarly consensus, and three characteristics about which there is substantial disagreement. You should bear these in mind as you work through the book. In the final chapter – when you are better able to evaluate them – there is a series of scholarly assessments of Charles I which you can consider in the light of your work in Chapters 1–6. The bibliography at the end is intended to help you to take particular aspects further.

First, here are the three aspects of Charles I that most historians have noted:

1 Privacy   All those who have written a biography of Charles have found him hard to get to know. Many monarchs have left us collections of papers and correspondence that reveal their beliefs. Charles' father, King James I, is such a person. But Charles was a deeply reserved ruler who found it hard to express his feelings, even to those around him. In 1628, for example, Charles was attending a religious ceremony when he learned of the murder of his closest adviser, the Duke of Buckingham. He remained in his seat impassively until the service ended, and then locked himself in his private chamber for several days, seeing no-one, distraught with grief. He then emerged and resumed his normal round of duties with his normal self-control. Those close to him who have left us descriptions of him, seem only to be able to describe the externals – the properness of his manner, the formal politeness, the reserve. It is for this reason that we have placed such emphasis on the art and artefacts that were produced under Charles' direct patronage. It is in the values and aspirations which they incorporate that most historians believe Charles most readily let the mask slip, and revealed himself most fully to us.

2 Rectitude   Although Charles I's enemies were to call him a tyrant, a man who invaded the liberties of his subjects, he does not stand comparison with the great wilful tyrants of history: the Emperors Tiberius and Nero; Vlad the Impaler; Ivan the Terrible; Idi Amin. He did not have his political opponents murdered or tortured; nor did he deliberately subject them to rigged trials. He did not believe himself free to follow his every whim. He believed firmly that he was answerable to God alone for his actions, but he was a devout Christian who took that accountability to God very seriously. He did, of course, differ from many of his subjects in his interpretation of the circumstances in which he could use the prerogative or emergency powers with which he believed himself invested, but there is no evidence that he allowed greed, pique or other unprincipled feelings to dictate his conduct. He always scrupulously examined his conscience and only acted when he was convinced that he was within the rights conferred upon him by God and the law. His personal moral standards were high: he was one of the very few chaste kings in English history, and he imposed stricter standards of sexual and financial probity upon his ministers than anyone else until the reign of Queen Victoria. There was a prudish side to him: when Lord Castlehaven was being tried for rape and buggery in 1629, Charles issued a proclamation 'prohibiting all women to be present, upon pain of ever after being reputed to have forfeited their modesty.' He was severe in his application of the law, but not vindictive. While he was in Scotland, a laird was convicted of incest: Charles refused to grant a pardon, but ordered that 'the maintenance of his wife and children and the standing of his house be provided for'. He could be unforgiving of his political enemies, and could never accept that those who differed from him were acting in good faith, but he did recognize and reward repentance.

3 Decisiveness   Charles has been accused by many (not all) historians of inflexibility, but never of indecisiveness. He did not fail to grasp nettles or shirk responsibilities. He wrote to a Secretary of State in 1632, 'though second thoughts sometimes may come too late, yet for the most part they are the best'. It is generally held that in so far as this describes Charles' behaviour, he should have said 'usually too late' rather than 'sometimes too late'! Even when – as in deciding between peace and war with the Scots in 1638–40, or between conciliation of and confrontation with the Long Parliament in the winter of 1641–2 – he appears to have contradictory policies, most historians would argue that he was either deliberately keeping his options open pending a decisive leap, or that one of the policies was a smokescreen to disguise a pre-commitment to a hard-line decision.

These three areas of scholarly consensus can be matched by three issues upon which historical opinion is seriously divided:

1 Personal involvement in government   Some monarchs (e.g. Henry VII, or Philip II of Spain) were obsessively concerned with the minutiae of government. Others (like Henry VIII) were content to lay down the broad lines of policy and to leave ministers to work out the details. (Others left everything to their ministers.) It is not clear quite where Charles I lies on this spectrum of involvement. Something of the range of views can be seen in the following extracts from two scholars who have paid a great deal of attention to Charles in recent years, Charles Carlton and Kevin Sharpe.

(a)

Sometimes Charles displayed the occasional burst of energy. While
signing a routine letter, one of thousands written in his name, to St
Catherine's Hall, Cambridge, he noted the clerk had omitted to insert
the recipient's name and address, and so did so in his own hand. He
personally went through the lists of presents given and received at   5
New Year . . . But such clerical interventions were noteworthy only
for their rareness and a pettifogging concern for trivia. The King
seldom bothered himself with the tens of thousands of petitions
addressed to the Crown. He might read some, and then act as a
postman who sorted them to the appropriate minister, whose   10
recommendation he invariably accepted . . . In January 1636,
Windebank sent him a list of items that urgently required the King's
attention, ranging from diplomatic decisions to the naturalizations of
denizens. The King's annotations betrayed that he was neither
interested in, nor knowledgeable about, these subjects . . . Charles   15
was as indolent in dealing with his 'out' correspondence as he was
with his 'in', admitting on several occasions to his good friend
Hamilton 'you know that I am lazy enough in writing.' Thus it seems
reasonable to conclude that compared to any other Tudor or Stuart
monarch a higher proportion of acts done in Charles' name were   20
done either without his knowledge or initiative . . . Charles did not
work hard at winning his subjects' loyalty. He preferred the pleasure
of hunting from county to county to the tedium of state visits, with
long addresses from petty worthies.

C. Carlton, *Charles I*, 1983, p. 158

(b)

[After Buckingham's death] no minister emerged to enjoy a monopoly
of either patronage or influence over royal policy . . . Charles
eschewed the advice of favourites and restored an active Privy
Council to its traditional position as adviser to the King and the
principal executive body. After 1628 Charles had no first minister.   5
The new formality at Court distanced the King and so excluded most
courtiers from developing the close relationship with Charles that
Buckingham had enjoyed . . . Charles I, as Clarendon and Secretary
Dorchester concurred, 'resolved to hold the reins in his own hands

and put no further trust in others than was necessary for the capacity   10
they served in'. But Personal Rule was not autocratic government.
Charles attended the Privy Council more often; he carefully pondered
advice. Evidently, he attempted to strengthen the Council's authority
and usefulness by adding to its numbers those who might bring their
own knowledge and influence to the board.

K. Sharpe, 'Crown, Parliament and the Localities' in *English
Historical Review,* **1986**

(c)

What were the ideals and purposes . . . which underlay the directives
and proclamations issued and published by king and Council during
the decade of Personal Rule? . . . The language of the king's own
letters and speeches, the articulation made by his hand to official
papers, the comparison of documents passing through the Signet   5
Office with the business reported in the Council register enable us to
form a fairly clear picture of what mattered most to Charles. Central
to all his directives was an obsessive concern with order – in matters
both large and small.

K. Sharpe, 'The Personal Rule of Charles I' in *Before the English
Civil War 1603–42,* **H. Tomlinson (ed.), 1983, pp. 58–9**

2 Public and private rhetoric   Because Charles was such a private man;
because he committed less to paper than most early modern monarchs;
and because most of his formal speeches and proclamations were either
ghosted for him by his advisers, or written in consultation with them, it is
not only difficult to get at the man himself, but it is peculiarly difficult to
sort out the public stance from the private belief. How *privately* sympathetic was Charles to Catholics and Catholicism? Did he believe, as he
claimed, that his religious policies were grounded upon the religious
Settlement of 1559, or did he say so to reduce resistance to the new
directions in which he was leading the Church of England? Did he really
believe that a few 'incendiaries' and 'fiery spirits' were responsible for the
failure of successive parliaments; or was this a way of distracting attention
from his determination to get his own way however much the people at
large disliked obeying him?

3 Innovation   This is the nub issue, and it grows out of the previous point
(2). Critics of Charles I, both in the 1620s and the early 1640s, adamantly

maintained that his ministers were seeking to change the relationship of the Crown and the law, to enhance the authority of the Crown at the expense of civil liberties and the subjects' security in their property, and that he was tolerating if not sponsoring change in the beliefs and practices of the established Church. Charles consistently denied these charges, and counter-charged his critics with seeking to weaken the Crown and destroy the established Church. Historians have taken sides on this issue as freely as contemporaries did. This is an issue which the documents in this book should help you to decide – one way or the other – for yourselves.

1 Duke of York and Prince of Wales 1600–25

Charles I was born a week before Christmas in the year 1600, the second son and third surviving child of King James VI of Scotland, heir presumptive to the throne of England. A weakling child, whose growth was stunted by early bouts of rickets and who grew up with a noticeable speech impediment, he seems to have found little place in the affections of his parents, and even less in their plans until the death of his strong, energetic, wilful elder brother Henry in 1612. This chapter will examine three factors in Charles' early life that are commonly held to have influenced his style of government after he became King in 1625. The first was his father's personality; the second was the impact of the death of Prince Henry; and the third was the towering influence in the years after 1617 of George Villiers, Duke of Buckingham, James I's protégé and lover, who was also to dominate the politics of the early years of Charles' reign.

James I was a scholar–king. But Henri IV's soubriquet for him – 'the wisest fool in Christendom' – draws attention to a lack of discretion and judgement that many (by no means all) at the time and since saw as accompanying that profound academic learning. There was dispute at the time too (as there is amongst modern scholars) about his political achievements, and how far those were offset by his uncouthness and vulgarity of manner, and tolerance of considerable sexual and fiscal corruption in and around his Court. Below are three assessments by his contemporaries. Document 1.1 is a withering indictment delivered in the 1640s by a would-be courtier Sir Anthony Weldon, dismissed for an ill-advised tract against the Scottish people. Document 1.2 is from the memoirs, written in the 1630s, of a Suffolk gentleman and antiquarian, Sir Simonds d'Ewes, who had been brought up in London where his father was a judge. He was a Parliamentarian in the civil war. 1.3 comes from an account drawn up in 1607 by the Venetian ambassador in England and sent home to his masters.

1.1

He was a man of middle stature, more corpulent through his clothes than in his body, yet fat enough, his clothes ever being made large and easy, the doublets quilted for stiletto-proof, his breeches in great

pleats and full stuffed. He was naturally of timorous disposition,
which was the reason of his quilted doublets; his eyes large, ever   5
rolling after any stranger that came in his presence, insomuch as
many for shame have left the room, as being out of countenance. His
beard was very thin: his tongue too large for his mouth, which ever
made him speak full in the mouth, and made him drink very
uncomely, as if eating his drink, which came out of the cup of each   10
side of his mouth . . . His walk was ever circular, his fingers ever in
that walk fiddling with that codpiece; he was very temperate in his
exercises and in his diet, and not intemperate in his drinking . . . In
his diet, apparel, and journeys, he was very constant; in his apparel so
constant as by his goodwill he would never change his clothes until   15
worn out to very rags . . .

He was ever best when furthest from his queen, and that was
thought to be the first grounds of his often removes which afterwards
proved habitual . . .

He naturally loved not the sight of a soldier, nor of any valiant   20
man . . .

He was very liberal of what he had not in his own grip . . . and
had much use of his subjects' purses, which bred some clashings with
them in parliament, yet would always come off and end with a sweet
and plausible close . . . He loved good laws and had many made in   25
his time . . . By his frequenting sermons he appeared religious [yet]
he would make a great deal too bold with God in his passion, both in
cursing and swearing and one strain higher verging on blasphemy;
but would in his better temper say 'he hoped God would not impute
them as sins and lay them to his charge, seeing they proceeded from   30
passion.' He had need of great assurance, rather than hopes, that
would make daily so bold with God . . .

He was infinitely inclined to peace, but more out of fear than
conscience, and this was the greatest blemish this king had through
all his reign, otherwise [he] might have been ranked with the very   35
best of our kings . . . In a word he was (take him altogether and not
in pieces) such a king, I wish this kingdom have never any worse on
the condition, not any better. For he lived in peace, died in peace,
and left all his kingdom in a peaceable condition with his own motto
Beati pacifici [= blessed are the peacemakers].

Modernized version of an extract from Sir Anthony Weldon,
Character of King James, **printed in** *Secret History of the Court*, **anon,**
Edinburgh, 1811, vol. II, pp. 1–12

1.2

The royal corpse was interred on Saturday, May the 7th ensuring
[1625] . . . It did not a little amaze me to see all men generally slight
and disregard the loss of so mild and gentle a prince, which made me
even then to fear that the ensuing times might yet render his loss
more sensible, and his memory more dear unto posterity. For though   5
it cannot be denied but that he had his vices and deviations, and that
the true Church of God was well near ruined in Germany, whilst we
sat still and looked on; yet, if we consider his virtues and learning on
the other hand, his care to maintain the doctrine of the Church of
England pure and sound, his opposition against James Arminius and   10
other blasphemous Anabaptists, and his augmenting the liberties of
the English rather than oppressing them by any unlimited or illegal
taxes and corrosions, we cannot but acknowledge that his death
deserved more sorrow and condolement from his subjects than it
found.

The Autobiography of Sir Simonds d'Ewes, Bart, ed. J. O. Halliwell,
1845, vol. I, pp. 264–5

1.3

He is tall, of a noble presence, his physical constitution robust, and
he is at pains to preserve it by taking much exercise at the chase,
which he passionately loves, and uses not only as a recreation, but as
a medicine. For this he throws off all business, which he leaves to his
Council and to his ministers. And so one may truly say that he is   5
Sovereign in name and in appearance rather than in substance and
effect. This is the result of deliberate choice, for he is capable of
governing, being a prince of intelligence and culture above the
common . . .

   He is a protestant as it is called; that means a mixture of a number 10
of religions; in doctrine he is Calvinistic, but not so in politics . . .
The King is a bitter enemy of our [Roman Catholic] religion . . . he
is all the harsher because this last conspiracy against his life seems to
him, as it is in fact, the most horrible and inhuman that was ever
heard of. He said himself that the murder of a king had happened   15
before, the extinction of a House had been dreamed of, but the ruin
of a whole kingdom along with the King and his offspring, that was

without parallel . . . He has no inclination to war, nay is opposed to
it, a fact that little pleases them . . . He does not caress the people
nor make them that good cheer the late Queen did, whereby she won 20
their loves.

**Nicolo Molin, Venetian ambassador in London, to the Doge and
Senate in Venice, undated but from 1607, printed in** *Calendar of
State Papers Venetian 1603–7*, **pp. 509–14**

Questions

1 What is being referred to in the following phrases:
   (i) 'quilted for stiletto-proof' [1.1, line 3]
   (ii) 'the true Church of God was well near ruined in Germany' [1.2, line 7]
   (iii) 'James Arminius and other blasphemous Anabaptists' [1.2, lines 10–11]
   (iv) 'in doctrine he is Calvinistic, but not so in politics' [1.3, line 11]
   (v) 'this last conspiracy against his life' [1.3, line 13]?
2 Speculate what Sir Anthony Weldon might have been hinting at by saying 'he was ever best when furthest from his queen' [1.1, line 17]; and Sir Simonds d'Ewes by saying 'he had his vices and deviations' [1.2, line 6].
3 What do these three commentators [1.1–1.3] agree about in their view of James?
4 What do these three commentators disagree about in their view of James?
5 Document 1.1 was written in the 1640s, 1.2 was written in the 1630s, and 1.3 in 1607 by a foreign Catholic. To what extent does this affect your judgement of how far we can rely on the testimony of each?

The death of Prince Henry transformed Charles' life. From being unloved and ignored, he necessarily became the centre of attention. But neither his parents nor the people transferred their affections to him. Indeed it was several years before James could bring himself to confer upon Charles the title of Prince of Wales (which his brother had held from a much younger age). The following description of Prince Henry comes from Sir Simonds d'Ewes' autobiography [1.4]. Document 1.5 is representative of the fifty plus elegies published between 1612 and 1614 (including four anthologies from the universities and two volumes of funeral sermons).

1.4

The first public grief that ever I was sensible of was this year after
the death of England's joy, that inestimable Prince Henry. The
lamentations made for him was so general as even women and
children partook of it . . . He was a prince rather addicted to martial
studies and exercises than to golf, tennis or other boys' play; a true   5
lover of the English nation, and a sound Protestant, abhorring not
only the idolatry, superstition and bloody persecutions of the Romish
synagogue, but being free also of the Lutheran leaven . . . He
esteemed not buffoons and parasites nor vain swearers and atheists,
but learned and godly men . . . for the dear companions of his life.   10
So as had not our sins caused God to take him from us so peerless a
prince, it was very likely that popery would have been well purged
out of Great Britain and Ireland by his care; and that the Church of
God had not suffered such shipwreck abroad as it hath done for near
upon the sixteen years last past. Charles, his younger brother, our   15
present sovereign, was then so young and sickly, as the thought of
their enjoying him did nothing at all to alienate or mollify the
people's mourning.

The Autobiography of Sir Simonds d'Ewes, Bart, ed. J. O. Halliwell,
1845, vol. I, pp. 48–9

1.5

But our young Henry, armed with all the arts
That suit with Empire, and the gain of hearts
Bearing before him fortune, power, and love,
Appeared first in perfection, fit to move
Fixed admiration; though his years were green,   5
Their fruit was yet mature: his care had been
Surveying India, and implanting there
The knowledge of that God which he did fear:
And even now, though he breathless lies, his sails
Are struggling with the winds, for our avails   10
T'Explore a passage hid from human tract
Will fame him in the enterprise or fact . . .

Thomas Campion, *Songs of Mourning*, 1614

Questions

1   Why might d'Ewes have stressed that Prince Henry 'was a prince rather addicted to martial studies and exercises than to golf, tennis or other boys' play' [**1.4, lines 4–5**]?

2   What is implied by the phrase 'free also of the Lutheran leaven' [**1.4, line 8**]?

3   Document **1.4** was written after Charles I became King. Does that change its significance for the historian?

4   Do you consider that poems such as **1.5** offer evidence about Henry's reputation and 'a national sense of loss'?

5   Henry's death generated more elegies like **1.5** than any other death in the period. What might explain this fact?

After Henry's death, King James became more and more dependent on dashing young men about the Court who had the good looks, wit and flair which his younger son, a stammering, frail runt who had survived as stronger siblings died, lacked. The most important of these young men was George Villiers, by the end of the reign Duke of Buckingham. Initially Charles, jealous of this new call on his father's affections, set out to cross the favourite (turning on a water fountain and drenching the Duke's new clothes, or throwing tantrums during tennis matches) but by 1620 he had come to share his father's emotional dependency (but emphatically not his father's infatuation) with the man they both called 'Steenie'. It was with Buckingham, therefore, that Charles made his first important move in British and European politics when Prince and Duke persuaded a reluctant King to let them set out incognito to Spain. This rash and audacious scheme was intended to complete lengthy negotiations for a match between Charles and the daughter of Philip IV. This in turn was intended to secure Spanish support for the restoration of the territories on the Rhine taken from the Elector Palatine, Charles' brother-in-law. Something of the relationship between James, Charles and 'Steenie' at this time can be gauged from a letter written in 1623 [**1.6**]; while a more sanguine view of their expedition can be found in the report of the Venetian ambassador in London to the Doge and Senate in Venice [**1.7**].

1.6

Dear Dad and Gossip,

On Friday last we arrived here . . . The next morning we sent for Gondomar[1] who went presently to the Count of Olivares[2], and as speedily got me and your dog Steenie a private audience with the

King . . . To conclude, we find the Count of Olivares so overvaluing   5
of our journey, that he is so full of real courtesy, that we can do no
less than beseech Your Majesty to write the kindest letter of thanks
and acknowledgement you can unto him. He said, no later to us than
this morning that, if the Pope would give a dispensation for a wife,
they would give the Infanta to thy son's baby as a wench; and hath   10
this day written to Cardinal Ludovisio, the Pope's nephew, that the
King of England hath put such an obligation upon this King, in
sending his son hither, that he entreats him to make haste with the
dispensation . . . The Pope will be very loath to grant a dispensation,
which, if he will not do, then we would gladly have your direction,   15
how far we may engage you in the acknowledgement of the Pope's
special power; for we almost find, if you will be contented to
acknowledge the Pope chief head under Christ, that the match will be
made without him. So, craving your blessing we rest your Majesty's
humble son and servant   CHARLES   20

Your humble slave and dog   STEENIE

¹ Gondomar = a former Spanish ambassador in London
² Olivares = favourite and chief minister of Philip IV

Letter from Charles I, 10 March 1623, in C. Petrie (ed.), *The Letters
of King Charles I,* **1934, pp. 10–11**

1.7

It becomes more credible every day that the journey was pitched
upon in desperation as the last means whereby they could bring
about the desired conclusion of the marriage, in the assurance that
the Spaniards cannot send back the prince without a wife, detain him
without offence or injure him without hurting their own interests, as   5
if Spanish acuteness could not find plenty of ways and means,
detaining him without a wife but in hope of her, if it suited them, or
after giving her, if she became pregnant, drawing a thousand
advantages therefrom. There are some who believe, considering
Spanish methods and the prince's own disposition, that he may   10
become a Catholic, but they would not do this unless they aspire to
the evil of a civil war in the kingdom.

**Alviso Valonesso, Venetian ambassador in London, to the Doge and
Senate, 17 March 1623,** *Calendar of State Papers Venetian 1621–3,*
pp. 591–2

Questions

1   What does document **1.6** tell you about the relationship between James I, Charles and Buckingham?

2   Does document **1.7** convince you that the trip to Spain was a complete waste of time?

3   Does **1.6** provide evidence for the view in **1.7** that Charles 'may become a Catholic' [**1.7, lines 10–11**]?

This chapter concludes with some other glimpses of Charles in the years up to and immediately after his accession as King. Document **1.8** is a letter written to Buckingham in 1621, in which Charles comments on events in the Parliament then in session. In **1.9** there are extracts from a letter from Charles to the Pope during the excursion to Spain. **1.10** is an extract from the diary of William Laud, subsequently Charles' Archbishop of Canterbury. As far as we know this was written down at the time. Document **1.11** is drawn from the Venetian ambassador's report home just after James' death. Finally **1.12** is an extract from memoirs written after the Restoration (1660) by Lucy Hutchinson, the widow of a Parliamentarian colonel who had sat in the Rump Parliament after the execution of Charles I.

1.8

Steenie

The Lower House this day has been a little unruly; but I hope it will turn to the best; for, before they rose, they began to be ashamed of it. Yet I could wish that the King would send down a commission here, that (if need be) such seditious fellows might be made example to   5
others, by Monday next, and till then I would leave them alone. It will be seen whether they mean to do good, or to persist in their follies; so that the King needs to be patient but a little while. I have spoken with so many of the Council, as the King trusts most, and they are all of his mind, only the sending of authority to set seditious   10
fellows fast is my adding.

Thy constant, loving friend,

CHARLES P.

Prince Charles to Buckingham, 3 November 1621, in C. Petrie,
The Letters of King Charles I, **1934, pp. 5–6**

1.9

Your Holiness's letters I have received with no less gratitude and
reverence than that feeling of uncommon good will and piety
demanded . . . I will endeavour, that the peace and unity of the
Christian commonwealth, which hath been so long banished, may be
brought back . . . and to this same the inclination of my lord King   5
and father very much fires me . . . to put forth a helping hand to so
pious a work, as well as the grief which preys upon his royal breast,
when he weighs and ponders what cruel slaughters, what deplorable
calamities have arisen from the dissentions of christian princes . . .
The judgment your Holiness hath formed of my desire of contracting   10
affinity and marriage with the house of the catholic prince, is a test
both of your charity and wisdom; for never should I feel so earnest as
I do to be joined to any one living in that close and indissoluble
bond, whose religion I hated. Wherefore be your Holiness persuaded
that I am and ever shall be of such moderation as to keep aloof from   15
every undertaking which may testify any hatred towards the Roman
Catholic religion. Nay I will seize all opportunities . . . so that we all
confess one undivided Trinity, and one Christ crucified, we may be
banded together unanimously unto one faith.

Prince Charles, in Spain, to the Pope, 20 April 1623, in C. Petrie,
***The Letters of King Charles I*, 1934, pp. 15–16**

1.10

Sunday [1 February 1624] I stood by the most illustrious Prince
Charles at dinner. He was then very merry . . . Among other things,
he said that if he were necessitated to take any particular profession
of life, he could not be a lawyer; adding his reasons. 'I cannot,' saith
he, 'defend a bad nor yield in a good cause.' May you ever hold this   5
resolution . . .

Translated from an entry (in Latin) in the Diary of William Laud,
printed in W. Bliss (ed.), ***The Works of William Laud*, 1843, vol. III,**
pp. 146–7

1.11

The chief dispute among the courtiers is whether the household of
the dead king or that of the prince shall be the household of the

present king, but his Majesty does not wish to exclude his father's
old servants or abandon his own . . . The king observes a rule of
great decorum. The nobles do not enter his apartments in confusion   5
as heretofore, but each rank has its appointed place and he has
declared that he desires the observance of the rules and maxims of
the late Queen Elizabeth whose rule was so popular . . . the king has
also drawn up rules for himself, dividing the day from his very early
rising, for prayers, exercises, audiences, business, eating and sleeping   10
. . . The earl of Arundel has not profited by the proposals he laid
before the Council, which I find were under three heads – to
maintain the ancient nobility, not to put up offices for sale and that
the king should let his Council share the things which he wishes to
announce, publishing them as having been discussed with the   15
counsellors. His Majesty may take care that offices are not sold . . .
but the limitation suggested by Arundel did not please him . . . They
propose to perform the nuptials[1] in France . . . before the funeral in
this city . . . after which the bride will cross the sea . . . the king has
reissued the orders in favour of the Catholics, though they will have   20
to appear more moderate, as his Majesty seems devoted to his own
faith and has declared that he will give them protection, but not
liberty.

[1] The marriage referred to is the one Charles contracted with Henrietta-Maria, sister
   of Louis XIII of France, after the failure of negotiations with Spain

**Zuane Pesaro, Venetian ambassador in London, to the Doge and
Senate, 25 April 1625, in** *Calendar of State Papers Venetian 1625–6,*
pp. 20–1

1.12

The face of the court was much changed in the change of the King,
for King Charles was temperate, chaste and serious; so that the fools
and bawds, mimics and catamites, of the former court, grew out of
fashion; and the nobility and courtiers, who did not quite abandon
their debaucheries, yet so reverenced the king as to retire into corners   5
to practise them. Men of learning and ingenuity in all the arts were
in esteem and receiving encouragement from the king, who was a
most excellent judge and a great lover of paintings, carvings, gravings
and many other ingenuities, less offensive than the bawdry and
profane abusive wit which was the only exercise of the other court.   10

But as in the primitive times, it is observed that the best emperors were some of them stirred up by Satan to be the bitterest persecutors of the church, so this king was a worse encroacher upon the civil and spiritual liberties of his people by far than his father.

Lucy Hutchinson, *Memoirs of Colonel Hutchinson*, **Everyman edition, 1928, p. 67**

Questions

1   How far do documents **1.8–1.12** suggest that Charles had the same views as his father, and how far do they suggest that he held different views?
2   Do documents **1.9** and **1.12** affect your answer to question 3, page 15?
3   Does anything in documents **1.8–1.11** support Lucy Hutchinson's comment that Charles was to become 'a worse encroacher upon the civil and spiritual liberties of his people by far than his father' [**1.12, lines 13–14**]?

2 Early years 1625–9

Charles' early years as King were fraught ones. Foreign policy, religious policy and fiscal policy all generated heated debate in Parliament and the country of a bitterness not known since the 1580s. Initially most of the blame was laid on the head of Buckingham, but after he was assassinated by a deranged soldier in 1628, the King himself was inevitably exposed to more direct criticism. Some historians believe that we should stress the limited nature of the 'conflict'. Much of the protest in Parliament was initiated or amplified by noble factions seeking to discredit those in office in order to gain power themselves. This is something to consider as you read and discuss the documents in this chapter and in other reading. Here there is only space to let you examine some of the flashpoints.

Are we witnessing the ordinary stresses and strains within a fairly immature political system, inevitably generated by the demands of war? Are we seeing anger and frustration that is ephemeral, likely to dissolve with a return to peace in 1630? Or are we witnessing a conflict of ideas, of fundamentally opposed notions of government, so entrenched that they demonstrate that the country was ungovernable? If the latter is so, are we witnessing (1) a bid to enhance royal authority at the expense of political liberties; (2) a bid to increase parliamentary authority at the expense of the royal prerogative; (3) both; (4) neither? Was Charles wise or unwise in 1629 to embark on a prolonged period of non-parliamentary government? The documents below should help to elucidate these questions.

In 1624 Charles and Buckingham, after the humiliating failure of their Spanish adventure, persuaded a reluctant James to declare war on Spain. Their aim was to apply military and naval pressure on Spain so as to compel Philip IV to withdraw Spanish troops from the Palatinate. (England could never take on Spain single-handed, but the latter was already fighting on several fronts and was alarmed at the prospects of further escalation.) At the same time, Charles married Henrietta-Maria. The early years of the marriage were unhappy ones, and when both sides failed to honour some of the provisions of the marriage treaty, and when Louis XIII launched a military campaign to destroy the freedoms of his Protestant (Huguenot) subjects, Charles found himself at war with France too. While this war with two states, both more powerful than Britain, may seem

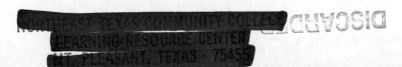

foolish and impractical to us, it should be stressed that there was little opposition to either war at the time. No Parliament between 1624 and 1629 was critical of Charles' objectives; but there was criticism of failures of execution – the humiliating failures of an Anglo-Danish expedition in 1624, of the Cadiz expedition of 1625 and the Île de Rhé expedition (to assist the Huguenots) in 1627. A majority in Parliament held Buckingham primarily responsible for these failures (and did not blame themselves for failing to supply the King's needs). Many Members would have preferred an essentially naval war, preying on Spanish shipping – their proposals much strengthened by the Dutch capture of the Spanish silver fleet in 1628.

Foreign policy failures were not in themselves, however, the main source of disagreement. More important were the financial policies employed to fund these policies. In 1626, for example, Parliament was willing to grant Charles most of the money he demanded (£300,000) on condition that he would dismiss and punish Buckingham (that is, accept their impeachment of him). Charles refused to do so and, to protect Buckingham, dissolved Parliament and lost his subsidies. He immediately demanded forced loans of an equal amount. He could point out that all his predecessors had required their subjects to lend money in times of military emergency; but it was clearly a provocation to demand them immediately after spurning a grant by Parliament. The following group of documents tells the story of the Loan. Document **2.1** gives us Charles' justification for seeking the Loan, and **2.2** consists of extracts from a sermon preached in favour of it – a sermon Charles himself commended and ordered to be printed. Document **2.3** tells what happened in Bedfordshire when the King's commissioners summoned the freeholders to contribute, and **2.4a** and **b** consist of extracts drawn from two bitterly hostile attacks on the Loan, written by an alderman of Canterbury, and an anonymous pamphleteer, probably living in Nottinghamshire.

2.1

When, with the advice of our Privy Council, We had resolved, for the necessary defence of our Honour, our religion, and kingdoms, to require the aid of our loving subjects in that way of loan, for the effecting whereof, our commissions are speedily to go out into the several counties & cities of this our realm; we have thought it fit to　　5 publish and declare unto all our loving subjects what our clear intention and royal purpose is thereby, that, whatever the occasions are, for the public cause both of religion and state, and how great soever, for the common defence (which are obvious to every man)

and no other possible and present course to be taken, nor this to be   10
avoided, if we as a King shall maintain the cause and party of
religion, preserve our own honour, defend our people, secure our
kingdoms and support our allies, all which we are tied to do by that
bond of sovereignty, which under God we bear over you.
Nevertheless, we are resolved . . . that this course, which at this time   15
is thus inforced upon us by that necessity, to which no ordinary
course can give the Law, shall not in any wise be drawn into
example, nor made a precedent for after times.

Royal Proclamation, 7 October 1626, in J. Larkin (ed.), *Stuart Royal
Proclamations, II, King Charles I,* **1625–46, 1983, pp. 110–11**

2.2

Subjects are bound to obedience by the double obligation of Justice
and of Necessity; except they will suffer as rebels or ill-doers, or
busy-bodies in other men's matter, as St Peter phraseth it. Or except
they will have that inconvenience granted, that the general laws or
government of a nation, must be dispensed withal according to the   5
particular conceit and apprehension of every private person – whereat
what toleration of heresy, what connivance at errors, what danger of
schisms in the church and factions in the state, must necessarily
follow, is easy to be conjectured . . . If princes command any thing
which subjects may not perform because it is against the laws of (1)   10
God or of (2) Nature, or (3) impossible, yet subjects are bound to
undergo their punishment without either resistance or railing or
reviling, and so to yield a passive obedience where they cannot
exhibit an active one . . . If a prince impose an immoderate, yea an
unjust tax, yet the subject may not thereupon withdraw his obedience   15
and duty. Nay, he is bound in conscience to submit, as under the
scourge of sin . . .
   Oh let us not then conceive to ourselves a Conscience grounded
upon suspicious conjectures; concerning which, no man can ever set
down certainties; and we are bound to believe the best concerning all   20
men, much more concerning sovereigns' promises . . . Oh let us not
therefore, I say, conceive to ourselves such scruples as not to give
tribute where and when tribute is due, or to refuse a loan, or any
other aid which is not unjustly exacted, and which is promised shall
not be immoderately demanded, especially considering that thereby,   25

we who are bound to lay down our lives for our brethren, may by
laying down a little of our estates, save our own lives.

R. Sibthorpe, *Apostolic Obedience*, 1627, pp. 8–19

2.3

Then his Majesty's letters were openly read, in the second place the
Instructions, and in the third place the letters of the lords of the
Council; and after, I being before designed to make a narration of the
state of the business and to further the same by reasons made
according to instructions agreed by the rest of the Justices and   5
delivered unto me, I did to the uttermost of my understanding
endeavour to perform their direction and set forth the business; after
which we departed, leaving the High Constable of every hundred[1] as
a fit man to further the business and appointing to return back about
two hours after. When we were ready to return back the High   10
Constables came unto us and made it known that . . . they found the
opinion and vote of every Hundred to be, not to give to His Majesty
but in a Parliamentary way . . .

   We [= the Justices] did divers of us speak with particular men in
the business, but we found them resolutely in the same opinion as the   15
high constables did report . . . A proclamation was [then] made that
all that would give should go to the right hand, and all that would
not to the left; whereupon all the whole company went to the left
hand . . .

   After which general declaration of every man's mind we did   20
expostulate with the high constables for the reason of this averseness
. . . and the reasons made and delivered were to this effect, that they
made some question whether this course now holden were not against
law, and they conceived it was not grounded upon good precedent
and they feared future danger by such a precedent. They much   25
insisted that the parliamentary way of raising money was most equal
and most indifferent . . . They alleged that, as the parliamentary way
of giving was most equal, so it did produce good effects, making good
law, redress of grievances if anything were amiss, pardons etc. And
they did declare that the general opinion was that in a parliamentary   30
way every man would be willing to contribute to his ability.

[1] hundred - administrative division of a county comprising a group of parishes

R. D. Gilmore (ed.), 'Papers of Richard Taylor of Clapham',
Bedfordshire Historical Records Society, **vol. XXV, 1947, pp. 107–8**

2.4a

Subjects may disobey and refuse an unworthy king's command and
request if it be more than of duty we owe unto him. Yea, gracious
subjects ought of duty in their places to discountenance and
dishearten graceless tyrants that will not kill Agag[1] but in his defence
fall out with Parliament, and with loans and impositions and exalted   5
services continue to deny right and liberty and to oppress and
exhaust the people . . .

[1] Agag = a King of the Amalekites who committed atrocities against the Jewish
people but who was pardoned by King Saul at the end of the wars. Saul's minister
Samuel, ignoring Saul's order, executed Agag. The context of the passage makes it
clear that Scott intends the reader to see Buckingham as a modern Agag

**Untitled and unfoliated work by Thomas Scott in Kent Archives
Office (U 951, Z10)**

2.4b

Be sure whatsoever is given out of Parliament will be cast away and
not dispersed for the good or safety of the Commonwealth . . . but
for the private uses and satisfying of the ambitious desires of
Favourites . . . [refusal] will be the only way to have a Parliament
whereby the bloodsuckers of the Commonwealth shall receive any   5
punishment.

**Anon, 'To All English freeholders from a Welwisher', Public Record
Office, SP16/54/821**

Questions

1   Summarize the arguments of documents **2.1** and **2.2** for paying the
Loan.
2   Summarize the arguments of documents **2.3** and **2.4a** and **b** against
paying the Loan.
3   Within six weeks of the meeting described in **2.3**, almost all the
money Charles was seeking from Bedfordshire had been paid, and, as
far as we know, few men had had to be arrested or otherwise
punished. Does this affect your judgement of **2.3**?
4   Documents **2.4a** and **b** come from the only two tracts (both
unpublished at the time, but circulated in manuscript) which we

know about which were critical of the Loan. Does this mean that
most people didn't feel strongly about the Loan?

5   Sibthorpe [2.2] was impeached by Parliament in 1628, but protected
and promoted by the King. Do you think that:
   (i) Parliament overreacted by impeaching him
   (ii) the King was wise or unwise to show him favour?

Although, in the end, Charles got almost all the money he had demanded,
it is clear that he had generated a lot of ill-will. The Council was divided
over the best course to be adopted towards refusers. The hardliners, headed
by Charles, wanted to mete out severe punishments – the wealthy were to
be imprisoned, the less wealthy to be impressed into the army or to have
soldiers billeted on them [2.5]. The moderates urged a more conciliatory
approach. The law officers pointed out to the King that he was faced by a
major difficulty: while all his predecessors had collected forced loans, they
had never had to punish anyone for refusing – the one thing loans had
never had to be was forced! The lack of precedents made the King's position
very doubtful. Thus when Charles went ahead and arrested a group of
leading gentry, he was faced by a legal challenge. Five knights sought a
writ of *habeas corpus*, which required their gaoler to satisfy the Court of
King's Bench that they were imprisoned for a 'cause known to the law'.
Rather than have his right to loans tested by the judges, Charles instructed
his lawyers to inform the Court that the knights were in prison 'by special
commandment of the king', that is, for reasons of State security which it
was not safe to make public. He was able to produce a string of precedents
for this 'prerogative' imprisonment. The judges were unhappy, but forced
to accept the precedents. They did, however, stop short of giving the King
the complete victory he wanted. They remanded the prisoners pending a
fuller hearing and entered this as a 'rule of court' rather than a judgement,
which weakened its use as a further precedent. The King was furious, and
ordered the Attorney General to amend the decision so that it was entered
as a binding judgement. This, together with the Loan itself, became the
centre of a political storm in the 1628 Parliament. The eventual outcome
was the Petition of Right, a formal parliamentary declaration which with
the royal assent attached, became as binding on the judges as an Act of
Parliament would have been. Yet, MPs were circumspect in reaching this
outcome. They were careful not to renew the attack on Buckingham or to
raise the issue of tonnage and poundage or impositions (see below) both of
which they feared would lead to another early dissolution. They proceeded
slowly and patiently, not precipitously. Documents 2.6–2.10 tell the story of
the 'Five Knights Case', and the subsequent debates over the issue of
freedom from arbitrary imprisonment in the Parliament of 1628. In order

to demonstrate the difficulty of reconstructing the debates of this period, which derive from the jotted notes taken down by other Members at the time, document **2.9** consists of all three known versions of one particular speech by Sir Robert Phelips.

2.5

Whereas . . . we did . . . require the aid of our good and loving subjects of that county [of Gloucester] by lending unto us such competent sums of money as might enable us to provide for our own and their safeties and for defence of the true religion and of our kingdoms and dominions . . . Forasmuch as we understand that 5
divers of them . . . have obstinately refused to assist us in this extremity thereby discovering their disaffection to their prince and county, and exposing them as much as in them lies to the foreign enemy. We having taken into our princely consideration the dangerous consequence of this refusal, do by the advice of our Privy 10
Council think fit that such as neglect us and themselves shall serve in person for the defence of our kingdoms. We do therefore hereby will and authorize you forthwith to press [= conscript] or cause to be pressed within our county of Gloucester one hundred and fifty of these persons to serve on foot in our wars according to direction, 15
which have refused to lend us such sums of money as have been demanded of them . . .

Draft letter from the King to the Commissioners of Gloucestershire, Public Record Office, SP 16/89/4

2.6

The Record [of the judgement in the Five Knights Case] read . . .

The draft of the judgement intended to be entered, and room left for it. The form unusual, drawn up by Mr Attorney General in Sir John Heveningham's case [= one of the Five Knights]. The report read and that draft also. 5

The Attorney [General said] that he did direct the Clerk to make this draft out of the duty of his place for the King. Though he had no direction, he called upon the Clerk often, being often called upon himself. And justified each part thereof . . . It came forth now by misfortune, and hath given much distaste, which I am sorry for. But 10 perusing the old precedents with these, I found no difference but a few words . . .

The Duke [of Buckingham said that] the Attorney [General] had a check from the King because he had not entered that draft.

F. H. Relf (ed.), *Notes of the debates in the House of Lords in 1628*, **Camden Society, 3rd series, vol. 42, 1929, p. 93**

2.7

Mr Keeling [clerk of the Court of King's Bench] who came this morning to the committee, and told them the whole proceedings, and brought that copy the clerk wrote out of, and said that after Michaelmas term last, the Attorney General wished him to make a special entry of the *habeas corpus*. He told him he knew no special   5
entry, but (said he) if you please to draw a note, and the court assent to it, I will enter it. The Attorney drew a note to that effect as it is now drawn up, and Mr Keeling, having the note, went to the judges, and at that time they would not assent to any special entry, but the Attorney divers times sent to him, and told him there was no remedy   10
but he must draw it, and a week before the parliament the Attorney called to him for it, and told him he must enter it . . .

R. C. Johnson and M. Jansson Cole (eds.), *Commons Debates, 1628* **(for 31 March 1628), vol. II, p. 229**

2.8

Mr Selden [said:] I do so verily believe that this order had been recorded but for the Parliament, as I do believe that it will be recorded yet so soon as Parliament rises, if it be not prevented.

Commons Debates, 1628 **(for 30 March 1628), vol. II, p. 219**

2.9

(a) Opinions, judgments, or precedents are but servants to parliaments, and not masters to control them. The private judgment of any cannot take away the statutes. Let them on the other side deny there is a law or an act of parliament, or let them explain them. Concerning that judgment intended in the late *habeas corpus*, I have   5

heard many arguments used to qualify that judgment, and that it was
no judgment. I believed them because I remembered the merit of
those judges that gave it, but if this record be true, and the act of the
court, give me leave to say it takes away all qualification. It
determines the question against us for ever and ever. I hope that it   10
was the draft but of some man that desired to strike us all from our
liberties. I hope the judges justly refused it, but if the judges did
intend it, we sit not here to answer the trust we are sent for if we
present them not to his Majesty to be punished. Let this be further
searched into, and let us see how this judgment lies against us, and   15
let it be recommitted and let the committee further examine the
matter and have power to send for records and parties.

(b) Advice to the other side: 1, Acts of Parliament; 2ly matters of
precedent; 3ly, opinion of the judges. Precedents are but servants to
acts of parliament. The judges may say what they will. Let them say
there is no such law, or apply it rightly. I know there is a member of
this House that hath some copies of their opinion, and I would wish   5
they might be produced. For the judges themselves I honour them.
But if this record of Mr Solicitor's be true, I suspend my opinion.
Otherwise, we sit here for justice, and I hope it shall never be denied
to us.

(c) Advice to those gentlemen that shall affirm and though it will
offer to be ruled by acts, precedents and opinions, neither opinions
nor precedents shall rule me against an act, for neither opinions nor
precedents, which are but servants to inform, are fit to contradict the
fundamental laws. Therefore they ought either to deny the laws, or   5
else to explain them otherwise than ever they have been. The record
which mentions Sir John Heveningham's case, if it be a judgment,
and so to be accounted, we are concluded as much as may be; and if
we sit here with any fidelity to the king or trust to the people and
ourselves, we have reason not only to question the proceedings of the   10
judges, but also entreat the king that they may have the judgment
and punishment that so great wrongers of the commonwealth have
merited. I desire the record may be seen and that will inform. I mean
the record or original from which the paper copy was taken.

**Three versions of a speech by Sir Robert Phelips made on 31 March
1628, in *Commons Debates, 1628*, vol. II, pp. 212, 218, 220**

2.10

Whereas it is declared and enacted by a statute made in the time of
the reign of King Edward the First . . . and by authority of
Parliament holden in the five and twentieth year of the reign of King
Edward the Third, it is declared and enacted, that from henceforth
no person shall be compelled to make any loans to the King against   5
his will, because such loans were against reason and the franchise of
the land . . . Yet nevertheless, of late divers commissions directed to
sundry Commissioners in several counties with instructions have
issued, by means whereof your people have been in divers places
assembled and required to lend certain sums of money unto your   10
Majesty, and many of them upon their refusal so to do, have had an
oath administered unto them, not warrantable by the laws and
statutes of this realm, and have been constrained to become bound to
make appearance and give attendance before your Privy Council, and
in other places, and others of them have been therefore imprisoned,   15
confined and sundry other ways molested and disquieted . . .
    And where also by the statute called 'The Great Charter of the
Liberties of England', it is declared and enacted, that no freeman
may be taken or imprisoned or be disseised [= deprived] of his
freeholds or liberties, or his free customs, or be outlawed or exiled; or 20
in any manner destroyed but by the lawful judgment of his peers, or
by the law of the land . . . Nevertheless . . . divers of your subjects
have of late been imprisoned without any cause showed, and when
for deliverance they were brought before your Justices, by your
Majesty's writs of *Habeas Corpus* . . . no cause was certified but that   25
they were detained by your Majesty's special command . . . and yet
were returned back to several prisons, without being charged with
anything to which they might answer according to law . . .
    Of late great companies of soldiers and mariners have been
dispersed into divers counties of the realm, and the inhabitants   30
against their wills have been compelled to receive them into their
houses, and there to suffer them to sojourn against the laws and
customs of the realm . . .
    Commissions . . . have [been] issued forth, by which certain
persons have been assigned and appointed Commissioners . . . of   35
martial law . . . by pretext whereof, some of your Majesty's subjects
have been by some of the Commissioners put to death . . .
    [The following paragraph calls upon the King to declare that

henceforth no loans shall be demanded, no person imprisoned
without cause shown, no soldiers billeted on civilians and no   40
commissions of martial law used against civilians.]

All which they most humbly pray of your Most Excellent Majesty
as their rights and liberty according to the laws and statutes of this
realm.

The Petition of Right, 1628, in S. R. Gardiner, *Constitutional
Documents of the Puritan Revolution*, **3rd edn, 1902, pp. 66–9**

Questions

1   The draft letter from Charles I [2.5] caused a long debate in the
Privy Council and it was finally decided not to send it. What would
have been the arguments for and against the proposed course of
action?

2   Attempt to reconstruct Attorney General Heath's argument from the
sketchy notes taken down by an observer [2.6].

3   Why might Keeling have been so reluctant to obey the Attorney
General's instruction [2.7]?

4   Why did Heath's actions cause so much alarm in Parliament [2.8–
2.10]?

5   Buckingham's intervention referred to in 2.6 has been called 'a very
grave error of judgement'. Do you agree?

6   Document 2.9 consists of the notes taken by three different Members
of a single speech by Sir Robert Phelips. It is typical of the kind of
material historians of Parliament have to work with. Are you
reassured by the way the speeches are consistent with one another, or
alarmed at their differences one from another? Discuss the
implications for the way historians write about the history of
Parliament in this period.

7   From the documents so far in this chapter, can either the Crown or a
majority in Parliament be shown to be seeking to change the
Constitution? Consider the implications of your answer.

8   How far would you accept the judgement of the historian who
described the Petition of Right [2.10] as a document which 'secured
liberties and reduced the risk of royal tyranny'?

Neither the Petition of Right nor the assassination of Buckingham shortly
afterwards ended Charles' difficulties with Parliament. In the following

session, new grievances were raised and Charles, feeling he could not get the support he felt he was entitled to, determined to dissolve Parliament. Learning of his intention, a minority of furious Members physically restrained the Speaker (a Crown nominee) in his seat (once he rose from it the House would be adjourned) and passed a series of motions collectively known as 'The Protestation' [2.11]. The motions were concerned with religion (see Chapter 4) and Charles' collections of customs duties.

The background to the complaint about customs duties was as follows. Every ruler for 200 years had been granted tonnage or poundage for life by his or her first Parliament. James I had sought to augment his customs revenues by prerogative action, by placing surcharges ('impositions') on imported and exported goods. This had provoked arguments in the Parliaments of 1610 and 1614 (and to a lesser extent 1621). In 1625, Charles' first Parliament had delayed the grant of tonnage and poundage until a compromise could be reached (ie. an increased parliamentary grant in exchange for a promise that there would be no further impositions). Other events such as those discussed above had kept the subject of customs and impositions off the parliamentary agenda in both 1626 and 1628. Meanwhile Charles I had continued to collect both.

Once the third Parliament was dissolved, Charles arrested the ringleaders of the protest. Historians are divided over whether he made an immediate decision not to meet Parliament again for the foreseeable future. It may have been an option that hardened into a resolve only by about 1632. Some light on his view of the political situation is to be found in document **2.12**, drawn from his declaration issued after the dissolution of Parliament.

2.11

1 Whosoever shall bring in innovation in religion, or by favour or countenance seek to extend or introduce Popery or Arminianism[1], or other opinion disagreeing from the true and orthodox church, shall be reputed a capital enemy to this Kingdom and Commonwealth.

2 Whosoever shall counsel or advise the taking and levying of the   5
subsidies of Tonnage and Poundage, not being granted by
Parliament, or shall be an actor or instrument therein, shall be
likewise reputed an innovator in the Government, and a capital
enemy to this Kingdom and Commonwealth.

3 If any merchant or person whatsoever shall voluntarily yield, or   10
pay the said subsidies of Tonnage and Poundage, not being granted

by Parliament, he shall likewise be reputed a betrayer of the liberties
of England and an enemy to the same.

[1] Anti-Calvinist doctrine which grants some men a role in attaining or forfeiting
salvation to Eternal Life (See Chapter 4)

**Protestation of the House of Commons, 2 March 1629, in S. R.
Gardiner,** *Constitutional Documents of the Puritan Revolution,* **1902,
pp. 82–3**

2.12

Howsoever princes are not bound to give an account of their actions,
but to God alone; yet for the satisfaction of the minds and affections
of our loving subjects, we have thought good to set thus much down
by way of declaration, that we may appear to the world in the truth
and sincerity of our actions . . . We are not willing to derogate from   5
the merit and good intentions of those wise and moderate men of that
House . . . so we must needs say that the delay of passing the
[subsidy bill], occasioned by causeless jealousies stirred up by men of
another temper, did much lessen both the reputation and reality of
that supply: and their spirit, infused into many of the commissioners   10
and assessors in the country hath returned up the susidies in such a
scanty proportion, as is infinitely short, not only of our great
occasions, but of the precedents of former subsidies, and of the
intentions of all well-affected men in that House . . .
  As we have been careful for the settling of religion and quieting   15
the church, so were we not unmindful of the preservation of the just
and ancient liberties of our subjects, which we secured to them by
our gracious answer to the Petition [of Right] in Parliament, having
not since that time done any act whereby to infringe them; but our
care is, and hereafter shall be, to keep them entire and inviolable . . .   20
No sooner, therefore, was the parliament set down, but ill-affected
men began to sow and disperse their jealousies, by casting out some
glances and doubtful speeches, as if the subject had not been so
clearly and well dealt with, touching the liberties, and touching the
Petition answered the last Parliament. This being a plausible theme,   25
thought on for an ill purpose, easily took hold on the minds of many
that knew not the practice . . .
  We are not ignorant how much that House hath of late years

endeavoured to extend their privileges, by setting up general
committees for religion, for courts of justice, for trade and the like; a   30
course never heard of until of late: so as, where in former times the
Knights and Burgesses were wont to communicate to the House such
business as they brought from the countries; now there are so many
chairs erected, to make inquiry upon all sorts of men, where
complaints of all sorts are entertained, to the unsufferable disturbance   35
and scandal of justice and government, which, having been tolerated
a while by our father and ourself, hath daily grown to more and more
height . . .

In these innovations (which we shall never permit again) they
pretended indeed our service, but their drift was to break, by this   40
means, through all respects and ligaments of government, and to
erect a universal over-swaying power to themselves, which belongs
only to us, and not to them . . .

And now that our people may discern that these provocations of
evil men (whose punishments we reserve to a due time) have not   45
changed our good intentions to our subjects, we do here profess to
maintain the true religion and doctrine established in the Church of
England without admitting or conniving at any backsliding either to
Popery or schism. We do also declare that we will maintain the
ancient and just rights and liberties of our subjects . . . Yet let no   50
man hereby take the boldness to abuse that liberty, turning it to
licentiousness; nor misinterpret the Petition by perverting it to a
lawless liberty, wantonly or frowardly, under that or any other
colour, to resist lawful or necessary authority. For as we well
maintain our subjects in their just liberties, so we do and will expect   55
that they yield as much submission and duty to our royal
prerogatives, and as ready obedience to our authority and
commandments, as hath been promised to the greatest of our
predecessors.

Declaration of Charles I, published 10 March 1629

Questions

1   'A gesture of frustration and anger, but little more'. Does this seem a
     fair assessment of the Protestation [2.11]?

2   (i) What is likely to have been meant or implied by the phrase 'shall
          be likewise reputed . . . a capital enemy to this Kingdom and
          Commonwealth' [2.11, lines 7–9]?

(ii) Do you suppose that Charles I was thought to be amongst the 'whosoever' referred to in **2.11**?

3 How convincing do you find the argument in Charles' Declaration [**2.12**]?

4 Would the framers of **2.11** have found anything in **2.12** they could agree with?

5 Do these documents [**2.11** and **2.12**] support the view that England was close to civil war in 1629?

6 Do the documents in this chapter suggest that England was ungovernable by 1629; that it was just badly governed; or neither?

7 Put yourself in the position of a Privy Councillor in 1629. Would you advise the King to embark on a period of rule without Parliament or not? If you answer yes, how would you justify your advice? If no, how would you have counselled him to secure better relations with future Parliaments?

3 The culture of the Court

Charles I was a deeply private man. All his biographers – and contemporaries – found him aloof and deeply reserved. Charles in turn found human relationships difficult, and he has left us little in the way of personal utterances. We can read his public statements, but they were all ghosted for him, and even if the message was his, we can never be sure how far they reflected *his* view of what he wanted his audience to hear. But he was also a man who cared passionately about the arts and about the rituals of kingship. Here, perhaps, his true personal preferences and yearnings can be glimpsed. He was, to a greater degree than any other monarch in English history, a patron of artists and musicians, of playwrights and architects. But for the civil war there would have been a new royal palace built at Whitehall which would have proved as much a personal statement of Charles' views of monarchy as the *Escorial* was a testament to Philip II's conception of absolutism, or *Versailles* to Louis XIV's. Preliminary sketches for the new palace had already been drawn during the early years of his reign.

Charles was a sensitive, appreciative and discriminating patron of the arts. Estimates suggest a collection of over 1,700 paintings and sculptures by 1649. Agents like Daniel Nys, Philip Burlamachi and Nicholas Lanier, and other connoisseurs such as Buckingham and the Earl of Arundel, collected for Charles all over Europe. They were constantly alert for works of art coming on the market (and not above *taking* them either: Sir Thomas Roe was instructed to climb the Golden Gate at Constantinople to chip reliefs off it for Arundel or Buckingham!).

Warrants to pay agents like Burlamachi and Lanier occur frequently in the *State Papers*. In June 1626, for example, £2,000 was paid to Lanier 'for pictures bought in Italy for the King's use'. When the Gonzaga dukes of Mantua were rumoured to be selling their enormous and prestigious collection, Charles was quickly informed, and bought the collection in 1628 for about £18,000. It consisted of 175 paintings, including, according to contemporaries, 19 Titians, 15 Guilio Romanos, 12 Montegnas and 10 Brueghels. Lanier played a key role in the purchase, even escorting the most valuable pictures overland to Flanders. Charles was later accused of 'squandering away millions of pounds on old rotten pictures and broken nosed marbles.' Most were disposed of after Charles' execution.

3.1 and 3.2 are two depictions of Charles I *à la chasse*. Painting 3.1 is by the Dutch artist, Daniel Mytens, who was prominent at Charles' Court from 1625 until the arrival of Van Dyck in 1632. The second painting [3.2] is by the Flemish artist Van Dyck, who had once worked as chief assistant to Rubens, and who was to hold a very prestigious position at the royal Court.

3.1   Daniel Mytens, *Charles I and Henrietta-Maria depart for the chase*, c. 1630–2

3.2

Van Dyck, *Charles I à la chasse*, 1635

Questions

1   Contrast the image of Charles I portrayed by Mytens [3.1] with that
     by Van Dyck [3.2]. Consider the following aspects:
     (i) the pose of the characters
     (ii) their facial expressions

(iii) their costumes
(iv) the expression and pose of the horse
(v) the background
(vi) what the *putto* (small angel) with flowers [3.1] might signify
(vii) the overall mood of the paintings

Painting **3.3** shows a portrait of Charles painted by Van Dyck a few years later.

3.3

Van Dyck, *Charles I on horseback*, c. 1638

Questions

1   In 3.3, what mood or image does Van Dyck achieve by:
    (i) the landscape
    (ii) the horse
    (iii) what Charles is wearing
    (iv) the King's posture
    (v) the Garter badge around his neck
    (vi) the expression on his face
    (vii) the inscription on the plaque fixed to the tree?

2   How may the features in Question 1 [(i)–(vii)] be linked with art
    historian Roy Strong's identification of the following aspects of
    Charles in the portrait [3.3]:
    (i) an Imperial prince – hero and emperor
    (ii) St George – saint and warrior
    (iii) Courtly love
    (iv) Divine Melancholy – calm spiritual contemplation
    (v) Philogenes – the wise King
    (vi) A Little God (cf. James I's *Basilikon Doron*) – 'the
        personification of all the virtues both as ruler and as a
        gentleman'. (R. Strong, *Charles I on Horseback*, 1972)?

3   Van Dyck, like the contemporary writers of masques, unites art,
    architecture and drama in an Arcadian or Classical setting. With
    reference to the material in this chapter, as well as your general
    reading, consider why might this have been so popular at the time.

During Charles' reign there were plans to replace the rambling assemblage of buildings which formed the royal residence at Whitehall with a monumental new palace. This palace was to incorporate the Banqueting House which had been built on the Whitehall site in James I's reign by Inigo Jones. Inigo Jones was Royal Surveyor and artistic adviser to the English Court; he was an architect, artist and designer of numerous masques and plays. Involved in the drawing up of the plans for the rebuilding of the palace was his assistant John Webb. Illustration 3.4 is one of many drawings of Whitehall Palace by Webb.

3.4

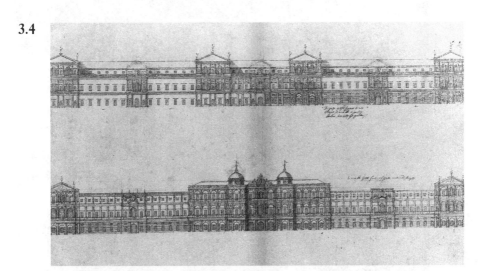

Design for Whitehall Palace, John Webb, c. 1638

The Banqueting House was designed to become an integral part of the new palace, and Charles commissioned some magnificent paintings for its ceiling. The paintings – almost certainly designed by Inigo Jones – were commissioned at a cost of £3,000 from Flemish artist Peter Paul Rubens and they reached London in 1635. Paintings 3.5–3.7 are the central panels on the ceiling. Around the three central panels are six smaller ones depicting Virtues destroying Vices – for example, Hercules vanquishing Envy. The paintings can still be seen today. Together they represent one of the greatest statements of absolute monarchy in Europe, and are a magnificent testament to Baroque art.

Rubens, *The Judgement of Solomon: James I recreates the Empire of Great Britain,* c. 1635

Rubens, *The Reign of Solomon: the Golden Age of James I,* c. 1635

Rubens, *The Ascension,* **c. 1635**

Questions

1   What image of kingship do you think the plan of Whitehall Palace [3.4] conveys?

2   Look at painting 3.5 and consider the significance of the following:
     (i) the two bare-breasted women supporting the crown
     (ii) the child between these two women
     (iii) the *putti* (small angels) carrying a coat of arms and a garland of red and white roses
     (iv) the *putto* setting fire to armour and weapons
     (v) James I's attitude
     (vi) the dome
     (the helmeted figure above the bare-breasted women is Minerva, or Pallas, who is linking the crown into one.)

3   Why do you think James I is compared to Solomon? It may help to consult the *Old Testament, I Kings 3, vv. 16–28*. With reference to this and your general reading, why did James I seem to excel Solomon in October 1604?

4   In what way did James's motto *Beati Pacifici* (Blessed are the Peacemakers) also link him to Solomon?

5   In painting 3.6, explain the significance of the following:
     (i) the three figures of a nude, a man brandishing a torch, and a many-headed hydra, being banished into the abyss
     (ii) James' gesture
     (iii) Minerva, or Pallas, with thunderbolt and shield
     (iv) Mercury, with winged helmet and caduceus (bottom left)
     (v) the two goddesses of Peace and Plenty

6   How might the vanquished figures [Question 5(i)] relate to rebellion (Gowrie 1600; and Gunpowder Plot 1605) or to the Pope as Antichrist?

7   With reference to painting 3.7, comment on the following figures around James as he ascends into the Empyrean:
     (i) Justice (with scales)
     (ii) Religion (a flaming altar)
     (iii) Faith (clasping a Bible)

8   Who would have seen these paintings [3.5–3.7] while the Banqueting House was in use as part of Whitehall Palace in the 1630s?

9   What do these paintings indicate about Charles I's view of monarchy?

The Masque was a lavish presentation of music, speech and dance, with elaborate costumes, scenery and stage machinery. Very popular under the early Stuart kings, Charles I and Henrietta-Maria often took part in masques with their courtiers. The Masque had a classical flavour, with gods, goddesses and allegorical figures expressing moral and political themes. The presence of the King and Queen in the Masque, frequently establishing order out of chaos by their very appearance, indicates Charles' view of his role in society. Notice how this role is presented in the following masque – William Davenant's *Salmacida Spolia*.

3.8

SALMACIDA SPOLIA

A MASQUE PRESENTED BY THE KING AND QUEEN'S MAJESTIES, AT WHITEHALL, ON TUESDAY, JANUARY 21, 1640

Discord, a malicious fury, appears in a storm, and by the invocation   5
of malignant spirits, proper to her evil use, having already put most
of the world into disorder, endeavours to disturb these parts, envying
the blessings and tranquillity we have long enjoyed.

These incantations are expressed by those spirits in an
Antimasque: who on a sudden are surprised, and stopt in their   10
motion by a secret power, whose wisdom they tremble at, and depart
as foreknowing that Wisdom will change all their malicious hope of
these disorders into a sudden calm, which after their departure is
prepared by a disperst harmony of music.

This secret Wisdom, in the person of the King attended by his   15
nobles, and under the name of Philogenes or Lover of his people,
hath his appearance prepared by a Chorus, representing the beloved
people, and is instantly discovered, environed with those nobles in
the throne of Honour . . .

The allusion is, that his Majesty out of his mercy and clemency   20
. . . seeks by all means to reduce tempestuous and turbulent natures
into a sweet calm of civil concord . . .

[After the Antimasque] the scene changed into a calm, the sky serene,
afar off Zephyrus appeared breathing a gentle gale: in the landskape
were corn fields and pleasant trees, sustaining vines fraught with   25
grapes, and in some of the furthest parts villages, with all such things

as might express a country in peace, rich and fruitful. There came
breaking out of the heavens a silver chariot, in which sat two persons,
the one a woman .. representing Concord: somewhat below her sat
the good Genius of Great Britain, a young man in a carnation   30
garment, embroidered all with flowers, an antique sword hung in a
scarf, a garland on his head, and in his hand a branch of [plane]
mixed with ears of corn: these in their descent sung together . . .

Song

CONCORD: 35

Why should I hasten hither, since the good
I bring to men is slowly understood?

GENIUS:

I know it is the people's vice
To lay too mean, too cheap a price   40
On ev'ry blessing they possess:
Th'enjoying makes them think the less . . .
Stay then! O stay! if but to ease
The cares of wise Philogenes.

CONCORD: 45

I will! and much I grieve, that though the best
Of kingly science harbours in his breast,
Yet 'tis his fate to rule in adverse times,
When wisdom must awhile give place to crimes.

Being arrived at the earth, and descended from the chariot, they . . .   50
departed several ways to incite the beloved people to honest pleasures
and recreations, which have ever been [special] to this nation.

BOTH:

O who but he could thus endure
To live, and govern in a sullen age,   55
When it is harder far to cure,
The People's folly than resist their rage?

. . . the King's Majesty and the rest of the Masquers were
discovered, sitting in the throne of Honour, his Majesty highest in a
seat of gold, and the rest of the Lords about him. This throne was   60
adorned with palm trees, between which stood statues of the ancient

heroes; in the under parts on each side lay captives bound in several
postures, lying on trophies of armours, shields, and antique weapons
. . . The habit of his Majesty and the Masquers was of watchet,
richly embroidered silver, long stockings set up of white; their caps   65
silver with scrolls of gold, and plumes of white feathers . . . there
came softly from the upper part of the heavens, a huge cloud of
various colours, but pleasant to the sight, which . . . open'd, and
within it was a transparent brightness of thin exhalations, such as the
gods are feigned to descend in: in the most eminent place of which   70
her Majesty sat, representing the chief heroine . . . The Queen's
Majesty and her ladies were in Amazonian habits of carnation,
embroidered with silver, with plumed helms . . .

The second dance ended, and their Majesties being seated under the
State, the scene was changed into magnificent buildings composed of   75
several selected pieces of architecture: in the furthest part was a
bridge over a river, where many people, coaches, horses, and such
like were seen to pass to and fro: beyond this, on the shore were
buildings in prospective, which shooting far from the eye showed as
the suburbs of a great city.   80
 From the highest part of the heavens came forth a cloud far in the
scene, in which were eight persons richly attired representing the
spheres; this, joining with two other clouds which appear'd at that
instant full of music, covered all the upper part of the scene, and . . .
beyond all these, a heaven opened full of deities, which celestial   85
prospect with the Chorus below filled all the whole scene with
apparitions and harmony . . .

Song

CHORUS:

So musical as to all ears   90
Doth seem the music of the spheres,
Are you unto each other still;
Tuning your thoughts to either's will.

All that are harsh, all that are rude,
Are by your harmony subdu'd;   95
Yet so into obedience wrought,
As if not forc'd to it, but taught.

The spheres passed through the air, and all the deities ascended, and
so concluded this Masque: which was generally approved of . . . to be
the noblest and most ingenious that hath been done here in that kind.   100

The invention, ornament, scenes and apparitions, with their
descriptions, were made by INIGO JONES, Surveyor General of his
Majesty's works.
    What was spoken or sung, by WILLIAM D'AVENANT, her
Majesty's servant.   105
    The subject was set down by them both . . .

**William Davenant, *Salmacida Spolia*, 1640, in *English Masques*,
(intro.) H. A. Evans, 1897, pp. 229–45**

3.9

**Design for final scene (lines 74–100) of *Salmacida Spolia*, John Webb,
1640**

3.10

Costume design for Charles I as Philogenes, Inigo Jones, 1640

Questions

1   Explain the references in the masque [**3.8**] to:
     (i) 'Amazonian habits' [**line 72**]
     (ii) 'music of the spheres' [**line 91**]
2   Why do you think Charles was cast as Philogenes in this masque?
3   What is the significance of the scene shown in **3.9** and in **3.8**, lines **74–100**?
4   Comment on the style of architecture shown in **3.9**.
5   What seems to be the essential message of the masque, and how effectively does it convey the atmosphere of England in the 1630s, especially the political situation in January 1640?
6   'The love of the king for the queen is mirrored in the love for his people, which in turn mirrors that heavenly love that binds the whole cosmos in universal harmony' (R. Strong). Discuss this view of the significance of *Salmacida Spolia*.
7   As an art form – part opera, part ballet, part drama – the Masque was chaste, disciplined and classical, but the spectacle mattered more than the content: 'nothing else but pictures with Light and Motion,' as Inigo Jones himself said. Do you agree?

8   How are aspects of this masque by Davenant and Inigo Jones
    [3.8–3.10] related to the paintings by Rubens [3.5–3.7] and Van Dyck
    [3.2 and 3.3]?
9   William Prynne wrote of 'those lascivious, whorish, or ungodly
    fashions and attires, which metamorphise and transform our light and
    giddy females of the superior and gentile rank, into sundry antique,
    horrid and outlandish shapes from day to day.' (*Histrio-mastix*, 1633)
    Whom do you think Prynne was specifically attacking, and how
    representative do you think his comments were?

Next we look at Charles' adaptation of the annual ceremonies of the Order
of the Garter (founded by Edward III in 1348, during the Hundred Years'
War, in celebration of English chivalry and in honour of England's patron
saint).

   The following documents begin with the view of Roy Strong, summariz-
ing his view of the new emphasis given by Charles [3.12]. There follow
extracts from *History of the Garter*, written by Elias Ashmole in 1715 [3.13
and 3.14], and from a contemporary *History of St George*, written by Peter
Heylyn, a presiding priest at the ceremonies of the Order, in 1631 [3.15].

3.11

Under Charles I there was a change of emphasis. Charles was less
interested in the use of the Garter as a public spectacle and more
preoccupied with its religious aspect. This was emphasized by the
removal of the festival to Windsor Castle away from London and by
the organization of Garter services as patterns of the new High   5
Church ceremonial so loathed by the Puritans . . .

R. Strong, *Charles I on Horseback*, 1972, pp. 59–60

3.12

King Charles I designed and endeavoured the most complete and
absolute Reformation of any of his Predecessors . . . The ceremonies
of the Feast Day may be divided into sacred and civil [processions, a
Feast, and several religious ceremonies, which reach a climax with the
offering of Gold and Silver and the Installation of new knights.] . . .   5
   The morning service having proceeded to the second lesson, . . .
the Prelate conducted the Serjeant of the Vestry from the Altar to his
seat. The knights [and others in due order] rise from their seats and
pass to the middle of the choir; and after the accustomed reverences,

go up to the sides of the altar . . . [then] the Gentlemen of the   10
Chapel . . . put on copes of cloth of gold and make themselves ready
. . . [then the nobility and the heralds approach]. Finally the
sovereign makes a reverence towards the altar and enters under the
Canopy [of gold and silver] which waits for him at the choir door . . .
They proceed with great devotion, singing the office appointed . . .

E. Ashmole, *A History of the Most Noble Order of the Garter*, 1715, pp.
455–70

3.13

[At the offering of Gold and Silver] The Organ begins to play and
forthwith a Groom and Page unroll a long carpet and spread it before
the Altar, which being done, the knights [etc.] ascend in usual order
and flank the carpet on both sides . . . The sovereign arises, makes
his reverence towards the altar, and then, descending, makes a little   5
reverence below, and ascends towards the altar with his attendants,
and being come to the middle of the choir, he makes another
reverence, and at the top step his last [reverence]. The sovereign
kneels at which instant Black Rod on his knees delivers His
Sovereign's [gold] offering to the senior knight and he, kneeling,   10
presents it to the sovereign which he immediately offers to the gold
basin.

E. Ashmole, *A History of the Most Noble Order of the Garter*, 1715, pp.
455–70

3.14

[Heylyn dismisses St George's battle with the Dragon as fantasy, but]
For the Dragon, if we understand the Devil, that old malicious
serpent . . . and [by] the combat betwixt our blessed martyr and that
monster, those many snares and baits which by the Devil were
provided to entrap him . . . [The Garter Badge recalls] to posterity   5
how bravely he repelled the Devil, how constantly he persevered in
the profession of his faith; the whole Church praying with him and
kneeling (like the Virgin) by him, in that holy Action, that God
would give him strength to subdue that evening, the dragon.

P. Heylyn, *A History of that Most Famous Saint and Soldier of Christ
Jesus; St George of Cappadocia . . .*, 1631, pp. 61–2

Questions

1   Why might Charles I have been 'less interested in the use of the Garter as a public spectacle and more preoccupied with its religious aspect' [3.11, lines 1–3]

2   What aspects of the ceremony 3.12 and 3.13 would have been 'loathed by the Puritans' [3.11, line 6]?

3   Would the Puritans have found anything objectionable in 3.14?

4   Do documents 3.11–3.14 add to or bear out the conclusions you have reached in discussing the earlier sections of this chapter?

Now look at the following photographs of coins which Charles I had issued. In an age before cinema, television and photography, these would have been the images of the King with which most people would have been familiar.

3.15

a   b

The inscriptions read:
 (a) CAROLUS D.G. MAG.BRIT.FRA.ET HIB. REX (Charles, by the grace of God, King of Great Britain, France and Ireland)
 (b) CHRISTO AUSPICE REGNO (I govern by Christ's protection)

Charles I Silver Crown, viewed on both sides, c. 1630, the Tower Mint, London

3.16

a   b

The inscriptions read:
(a) as **3.15a**
(b) (i) in the centre
   RELIG.PROT./LEG.ANG./LIBER.PAR
   (The Religion of Protestants/The Laws of England/The Liberties of Parliament)
   (ii) around the border
   EXURGAT DEUS DISSIPENTUR INIMICI
   (Let God Arise and Let his enemies be scattered [Psalm 68, as translated in the Book of Common Prayer])

Charles I Triple Unite, viewed on both sides, summer 1642, Oxford Mint

Questions

1   What image of himself is Charles presenting on the 'heads' side of these coins [**3.15a and 3.16a**]?
2   Why do you think that the inscriptions were in Latin?
3   Why might Charles have put a coat-of-arms on most coins up to 1642?
4   Comment on the contrasting messages in the centre and border of the 1642 coin [**3.16b**].
5   Why do you think coin **3.16** was struck in Oxford?
6   Do these coins confirm or conflict with the other evidence of Charles' self-image presented in this chapter?

Finally, consider how a modern historian, Kevin Sharpe, describes Charles I and his culture:

3.17

In many respects Charles I, more than any of his predecessors, was England's supreme Renaissance prince: his personal style (and within weeks that ordered for his court) was majestic, sophisticated and cultivated. The paintings of Van Dyck, vividly portraying a king calm and confident ruling unquestioned a country harmonious and   5 peaceful, encapsulate both the man and his vision of monarchy. Like the paintings, the court rituals and royal entertainments present the royal belief that the polity might be transformed into that ideal commonwealth by the power of the king's person and example.

K. Sharpe, 'Crown and Parliament' in L. M. Smith (ed.), *The Making of Britain: The Age of Expansion*, 1986, p. 51

Question

1   With reference to the sources in this chapter, do you agree with Sharpe's verdict [3.17]?

4 Charles, Laud and the Church

At Shrewsbury in late 1642, Charles undertook to 'defend and maintain the true reformed Protestant religion established in the Church of England.' In *Eikon Basilike*, his posthumous self-justification, the martyred sovereign included this advice to the future Charles II: 'Above all I would have you . . . well-grounded and settled in your religion, the best profession of which I have ever esteemed that of the Church of England.'

Although he was as devoted to the Church of England as Edward VI, Elizabeth or James I, Charles I was no bigot. He had no-one executed for their religious beliefs between 1625 and 1640, in contrast to the policies of all his predecessors since the Reformation.

Charles' religious policies are inextricably bound up with the name of William Laud, whom Charles rapidly promoted from the remote see of St David's to Bath and Wells, to London and (as soon as it was vacant, in 1633) to Canterbury (having promised it to him as far back as 1626). They appear to have seen eye-to-eye on all religious matters, and historians differ about who created the policies that caused such protests. Whether Laud carried out the King's ideas, or whether the King endorsed Laud's ideas, the outcome was the same.

After the tensions of Elizabeth's reign, with a Puritan minority demanding further reform of the Church and engaging in acts of passive disobedience (refusing to wear surplices, etc.), James I had brought relative religious peace and harmony. He had turned a blind eye to those whose consciences made them refuse to carry out all the rubrics of the Prayer Book, and the Puritans ceased organized attempts to change the way everyone else worshipped. There was a widespread recognition that if essentials of belief were agreed, then there could be latitude over matters of practice and worship.

It was this 'tolerance' which Charles and Laud were widely believed to have abandoned. Already in 1629, a majority of MPs were convinced that Charles had weakened in the fight against Popery and was engaged in sponsoring those who wished to change the beliefs and practices of the Church. These feelings are revealed in document **4.1**. Those who were accused by the House of Commons (and Charles himself), vehemently denied that they were changing the Church. They claimed that what they were doing was within the spectrum of belief and practice laid down in the Elizabethan Settlement of 1559. A letter from three bishops to the Duke of

Buckingham [4.2] makes this point and draws attention, like **4.1**, to another dimension of the bitter arguments which were to gather strength down to 1641 – the question of Richard Montagu. It followed the House of Commons' attempts to impeach Montagu, shortly to be made a bishop, for allegedly denying most of the doctrinal distinctions between Roman Catholicism and English Protestantism, and for denying Calvinist doctrines of predestination (ie. that God, since the beginning of time, had elected some men and women to salvation, and all others to damnation). Most MPs believed the Church of England to be committed to just such Calvinist doctrines. Montagu's anti-Calvinist teachings were labelled 'Arminian' since they were alleged to follow the teachings of a Dutch heretic called Arminius.

4.1

The dangers may appear partly from the consideration of the state of religion abroad, and partly from the condition thereof within his majesty's own dominions, and especially within this kingdom of England.

From abroad we make these observations: (1) By the mighty and   5
prevalent party by which true religion is actually opposed . . . (2)
Their combined counsels, forces, attempts, and practices . . . (4)
Their victorious and successful enterprises . . .

In his majesty's own dominions . . . here in England, we observe
an extraordinary growth of popery, insomuch that in some counties,   10
where in Queen Elizabeth's time there were few or none known
recusants, now there are above 2,000, and all the rest generally apt to
revolt. A bold and open allowance of their religion, by frequent and
public resort to mass, in multitudes, without control, and that even to
the queen's court, to the great scandal of his majesty's government   15
. . . The subtle and pernicious spreading of the Arminian faction,
whereby they have kindled such a fire of division in the very bowels
of the State as, if not speedily extinguished, it is of itself sufficient to
ruin our religion, by dividing us from the Reformed Churches
abroad, and separating amongst ourselves at home, by casting doubts   20
upon the religion professed and established . . .

The bold and unwarranted introducing, practising and defending
of sundry new ceremonies . . in conformity to the Church of Rome;
as, for example, in some places erecting of altars, in others changing
the usual and prescribed manner of placing the Communion table,   25

and setting it at the upper end of the chancel, north and south, in
imitation of the high altar . . .

The publishing of books and preaching of sermons, contrary to the
former orthodox doctrine, and suppressing books written in defence
thereof . . . That these persons who have published and maintained   30
such papistical, Arminian, and superstitious opinions and practices,
who are known to be unsound in religion, are countenanced,
favoured, and preferred: instance Mr Montagu, made Bishop of
Chichester . . .

**Resolutions on religion presented by a committee of the House of
Commons, 1629, in H. Gee and W. J. Hardy,** *Documents Illustrative of
the History of the English Church*, **1921, pp. 522–5**

4.2

May it please your Grace:

We are bold to be suitors to you in the behalf of the Church of
England, and a poor member of it, Mr Montagu, at this time not a
little distressed . . .

May it please your Grace, the opinions which at this time trouble   5
many men in the late work of Mr Montagu, are some of them such as
are expressly the resolved doctrine of the Church of England, and
those he is bound to maintain . . .

May it please your Grace further to consider, that when the clergy
submitted themselves in the time of Henry the Eighth, the   10
submission was so made, that if any difference, doctrinal or other, fell
in the Church, the King and the Bishops were to be judges of it . . .

But the Church never submitted to any other Judge, neither,
indeed, can she, though she would . . .

We must be bold to say, that we cannot conceive what use there   15
can be of civil government in the commonwealth, or of preaching and
external ministry in the Church, if such fatal opinions, as some which
are opposite and contrary to these delivered by Mr Montagu, are and
shall be publicly taught and maintained.

Fifthly, we are certain, that all or most of the contrary opinions   20
were treated of at Lambeth, and ready to be published, but then
Queen Elizabeth, of famous memory, upon notice given how little
they agreed with the practice of piety and obedience to all
government, caused them to be suppressed; and so they have

continued ever since, till of late some of them have received   25
countenance at the Synod of Dort. Now, this was a Synod of that
nation, and can be of no authority in any other national Church till it
be received there by public authority; and our hope is that the
Church of England will be well advised, and more than once over,
before she admit a foreign Synod . . .

JO. ROFFENS [= Rochester]
JO. OXON. [= Oxford]
GUIL. MENEVEN [= St David's]

**Letter from the Bishops of Rochester, Oxford and St David's to the
Duke of Buckingham, 2 August 1625, in W. Scott and J. Bliss (eds.),**
The Works of William Laud, Archbishop of Canterbury, **1847–60,
vol. VI, pp. 244–6**

Questions

1   Why was there so much concern with the 'extraordinary growth of
     popery' [**4.1, line 10**]?
2   Comment on the phrase 'the Arminian faction' [**4.1, line 16**].
3   Arminius was a Dutch Protestant. Why might a spread of his ideas
     divide 'us from the Reformed Churches abroad' [**4.1, lines 19–20**]?
4   Explain why the three bishops who signed letter **4.2** were concerned
     at parliamentary criticism of Richard Montagu.
5   Do you find that **4.2** supports the charges contained in **4.1**?
6   Document **4.1** makes it clear that following **4.2** Charles had appointed
     Montagu to a major bishopric. Can his decision to do so be defended?

There is no dispute that in the 1630s Charles I and Laud began on a
renovation of the Church. Laud undertook a visitation of the whole
Church, and sought to restore higher standards of obedience to the canons
of the Church. There is little evidence that he sought to introduce changes
for which there was no warrant in the canons and injunctions. But it is
widely accepted that he revived and attempted to enforce some practices
which had fallen into disuse and that he stressed some aspects at the
expense of others. There is no doubt too that he generated some very vocal
and strident opposition. But some believe that the cacophony was created
by a small minority while a majority acquiesced or quietly enjoyed seeing
the nose of the 'godly' put out of joint. However, the emphasis was on the
issue of instructions and exhortations; punishments were rare. Fewer
ministers were deprived or suspended in the 1630s than in most previous
decades since the Reformation (although more than one hundred minis-

ters, disliking what was demanded of them, voluntarily emigrated to
America and the Netherlands). Some brutal punishments were handed
out to those who published attacks on Laud and his policies (for an
example, see **4.16** and **4.17**) but they were very few in number.

Surprisingly, doctrinal issues were less prominent in the 1630s than in
the 1620s. Charles banned public debate of the disputed doctrines of
salvation and predestination, and both sides seem to have largely abided by
the rule. It is not possible to discover from his work what Laud himself
actually believed about salvation, though many historians believe that his
actions reveal a deep anti-Calvinism. Doctrinal changes did not figure
prominently in the charges brought against him by Parliament in 1641,
upon which he was tried, convicted and executed in 1644.

Greatest controversy surrounded the increased emphasis on ceremonial
aspects of worship. Document **4.3** shows how Laud justified his use of
ceremonies. It comes from an open letter to Charles I which Laud included
as a preface to a tract, in which he answered Roman Catholic criticisms of
the English Church.

4.3

This I have observed farther, that no one thing hath made
conscientious men more wavering in their own minds, or more apt
and easy to be drawn aside from the sincerity of religion professed by
the Church of England, than the want of uniform and decent order in
too many churches of the kingdom . . . It is true, the inward worship   5
of the heart is the great service of God, and no service acceptable
without it; but the external worship of God in His Church is the
great witness to the world, that our heart stands right in that service
of God . . . To deal clearly with your Majesty, these thoughts are
they, and no other, which have made me labour so much as I have   10
done for decency and an orderly settlement of the external worship of
God in the church; for of that which is inward there can be no
witness among men, nor no example for men. Now, no external
action in the world can be uniform without some ceremonies; and
these in religion, the ancienter they be the better, so they may fit   15
time and place. Too many overburden the service of God, and too
few leave it naked. And scarce anything hath hurt religion more in
these broken times than an opinion in too many men, that because
Rome had thrust some unnecessary and many superstitious
ceremonies upon the Church, therefore the Reformation must have   20
none at all; not considering therewhile, that ceremonies are the hedge

that fence the substance of religion from all the indignities which profaneness and sacrilege too commonly put upon it.

The Works of William Laud, vol. II, p. xvi

Questions

1 What would a Puritan have found unacceptable in document **4.3**?
2 Comment on the phrase 'the ancienter they be the better' [**4.3, line 15**].
3 'Laud was to the Church what Inigo Jones was to the Court.' Discuss.

One of the greatest flashpoints was the 'altar policy'. Down to the 1630s, most churches celebrated holy communion sitting round a 'communion table' which stood in the middle of the church. The priest brought the consecrated bread and wine to them as they stood or kneeled in a square. The Elizabethan injunctions permitted such an arrangement, but they also permitted the table to be left where it had been before the Reformation – against the east wall, with a rail around it, to symbolize that it was a 'holy table' or 'altar' (ie. a place of 'sacrifice') which only the priest could approach. Parishioners could then be made to come up in turn to kneel and to receive the bread and wine. Dispute in the 1630s was concerned with the name of the table, where it should stand, whether it should be railed, whether communicants should be required to kneel, and, not least, who had the right to determine these questions in each parish. This last question was settled by an order of Charles I in his Privy Council in 1633, in a test case brought over the Church of St Gregory, a church in the shadow of St Paul's Cathedral [**4.4**]. Documents **4.5a** and **b** sum up why those in Laud's circle preferred a railed-in east-end altar and **4.5b** illustrates the problems from one of Laud's annual reports to Charles (Laud himself did not insist on it in all cases, but he clearly *preferred* it in most churches). Document **4.6** shows that criticism of this policy was not confined to a Puritan fringe. It is drawn from a judgement delivered and published as a tract by John Williams, the Bishop of Lincoln. Drawings **4.7a**, **b** and **c** show the contrasting layouts of two churches built in the 1600s and the 1630s.

4.4

Now his majesty having heard a particular relation, made by the counsel of both parties, of all the carriage and proceedings in this cause, was pleased to declare his dislike of all innovation and receding from ancient constitutions, grounded upon just and warrantable

reasons, especially in matters concerning ecclesiastical orders and   5
government, knowing how easily men are drawn to affect novelties,
and how soon weak judgements may in such cases be overtaken and
abused. And he was also pleased to observe, that if those few
parishioners might have their will, the difference thereby from the
aforesaid mother church, by which all other churches depending   10
thereon ought to be guided and directed, would be the more
notorious, and give more subject of discourse and dispute that might
be spared, by reason of the nearness of St Gregory's, standing close
to the wall thereof. And likewise that for so much as concerns the
liberty given by the said Communion book or canon, for placing the   15
Communion table in any church or chancel, with most convenience,
that liberty is not to be understood, as if it were ever left to the
discretion of the parish, much less to the particular fancy of any
humorous [= self-indulgent] person, but to the judgement of the
ordinary [= the bishop], to whose place and function it doth   20
properly belong, to give direction in that point, both for the thing
itself, and for the time, when and how long, as he may find cause.
Upon which consideration his majesty declared himself, that he well
approved and confirmed the act of the said ordinary . . .

**Extracts from the Privy Council Register for 1633, in H. Gee and
W. J. Hardy,** *Documents Illustrative of the History of the English
Church,* **1921, pp. 534–5**

4.5a

For should it be permitted to stand as before it did, Church-wardens
would keep their Accounts on it, Parishioners would dispatch the
Parish business at it, School-Masters will teach their Boys to Write
upon it, The Boys will lay their Hats, Sachels and Books upon it,
Many will sit and lean irreverently against it in Sermontime, The   5
Dogs would piss upon it and defile it, and Glasiers would knock it
full of Nail-holes.

P. Heylyn, *Life of Archbishop Laud,* **1668, p. 289**

4.5b

1639   There happened . . . in the town of Tadlow [in Ely diocese] a
very ill accident on Christmas Day, 1638, by reason of not having the

communion table railed in, that it might be kept from profanations.
For in sermon time a dog came to the table, and took the loaf of
bread prepared for the holy sacrament in his mouth, and ran away   5
with it. Some of the parishioners took the same from the dog, and set
it again upon the table. After sermon, the minister could not think fit
to consecrate this bread; and other fit for the sacrament was not to be
had in that town; and the day so far spent, they could not send for it
to another town: so there was no communion . . .

Laud to Charles I, *The Works of William Laud,* **vol. V, p. 367**

4.6

That you should say you will upon your own cost build an Altar of
Stone at the upper end of your Quire [= Choir, or Chancel]: That
your Table ought to stand Altar-wise; That the fixing thereof in the
Quite is so Canonical, That it ought to be removed (upon any
occasion) to the body of the Church; I conceive to be in you so many   5
mistakings.

 For the first; If you should erect any such Altar, your discretion
would prove the only Holocaust to be sacrificed on the same . . . We
in the Church of England must take heed lest our Communion of a
Memory be made a Sacrifice.   10

 For the second point; That your Communion-table is to stand
Altar-wise; if you mean, in that upper place of the Chancel, where
the Altar stood. I think somewhat may be said for that, because the
Injunctions 1559 did so place it . . . But if you mean by Altar-wise,
that the Table should stand along close by the wall, so as you be   15
forced to officiate at the one end thereof . . . I do not believe that
ever the Communion-tables were . . . so placed in Country-churches
. . . The proper use of an Altar is to sacrifice upon, the proper use of
a Table is to eat upon . . . And because a Communion is an action
most proper for a Table, as an Oblation is for an Altar; therefore the   20
Church in her Liturgy and Canons calling the same a Table only, do
not you now, under the Reformation, call it an Altar . . . That it
should be there fixed, is so far from being the only Canonical way,
that it is directly against the Canon . . . And so is the Table made
removable, when the Communion is to be celebrated to such a place   25
as the Minister may be most conveniently heard by the
Communicants . . .

1 You may not erect an Altar, where the Canons admit only a Communion-table.

2 This Table . . . is not to stand Altar-wise, & you at the North   30
end thereof, but Table-wise, and you must officiate on the North-side of the same, by the Liturgy.

3 This Table ought to be laid up . . . in the Chancel only, as I suppose; but ought not to be officiated upon . . . but in that place of Church or Chancel where you may be most conveniently seen and   35
heard of all . . .

Your Parishioners must be Judges of your audibleness in this case, and upon complaint to the Ordinary, must be relieved . . .

J. Williams (Bishop of Lincoln), *The Holy Table, Name and Thing,* **1637, pp. 13–20**

4.7a

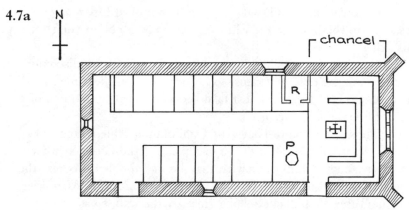

P = pulpit (shown in its probable original position)
R = reading pew
+ = altar (in the middle of the chancel)

Modern drawing of the plan of Langley Chapel, Shropshire, built c. 1601 as a chapel of ease in the parish of Acton Burnell.

4.7b

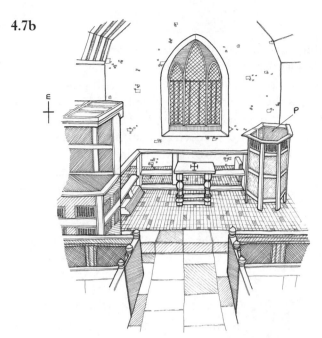

P = pulpit (shown in the position it stands today)   + = altar

Modern drawing of the interior of Langley Chapel, built c. 1601

4.7c

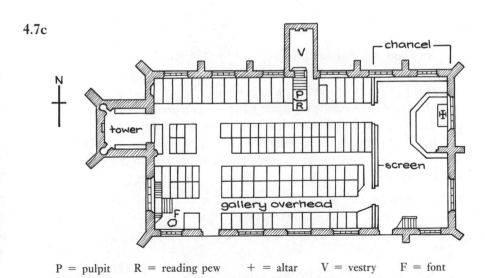

P = pulpit   R = reading pew   + = altar   V = vestry   F = font

Modern drawing of the plan of St John's Church in Leeds, built 1634, shown prior to the alterations of 1868

Questions

1   Why did Charles think that the physical arrangements of a parish church should be decided by the bishop rather than (as had been the custom) by the ministers and parishioners of each parish [4.4]?

2   In **4.5a** Heylyn defends the east-end railed-in altar, and Laud in **4.5b** illustrates his argument with a practical example. How would a Puritan have defended established practice against these arguments?

3   Is Bishop Williams in **4.6** flouting Charles' ruling in **4.4**?

4   What would Laud and Heylyn have found unacceptable in **4.6**?

5   Examine the sketches in **4.7**. What light do they shed on the issues in the 'altar dispute'?

6   Between 1633 and 1640 about 80 per cent of all parishes which did not already have altars fixed against the east wall built them. In 1641, acting on invitations from the House of Commons, 90 per cent of these new altars were removed. Comment on these figures.

Just as controversial was Laud's inhibition of preaching. He did not propose to prevent the long sermons that had become characteristic of English church services; but to reduce the emphasis on them. Document **4.8** represents his view on the proper balance, and **4.9** is drawn from the instructions he and the King issued in 1633.

4.8

> And you, my honourable Lords of the Garter, in your great solemnities, you do your reverence, and to Almighty God, I doubt not; but yet it is *versus altare*, 'towards His altar,' as the greatest place of God's residence upon earth. (I say the greatest, yea, greater than the pulpit; for there 'tis *Hoc est corpus meum*, 'This is My body;'   5
> but in the pulpit 'tis at most but *Hoc est verbum meum*, 'This is My word.' And a greater reverence, no doubt, is due to the body than to the word of our Lord . . .
>
> *The Works of William Laud*, vol. VI, p. 57

4.9

> V   That they likewise take great care concerning the lecturers within their several dioceses, for whom we give these special directions following:

1 That in all parishes the afternoon sermons be turned into catechising, by questions and answers, where and whensoever there is 5 not some great cause apparent to break this ancient and laudable order.

2 That every bishop take care in his diocese, that all lecturers do read divine service, according to the liturgy printed by authority, in their surplices and hoods, before the lecture . . . 10

4 That if a corporation maintain a single lecturer, he be not suffered to preach, till he professes his willingness to take upon him a living with cure of souls within that corporation, and that he do actually take such benefice or cure, so soon as it shall be fairly procured for him . . . 15

VII That the bishops suffer none under noblemen or men qualified by law, to keep any private chaplain in his house . . .

Instructions issued by Charles I and Laud in 1633, in E. Cardwell (ed.), *Documentary annals of the reformed Church of England . . .*, 1845, pp. 230–1

Questions

1 Why might Laud have felt more reverence for the altar than for the pulpit [**4.8**]?
2 Why were views such as those held in **4.8** controversial?
3 With reference to **4.9**, what were 'lectures'? Why might Laud have wanted only those who were ministers of parishes to be lecturers?
4 Why did the substitution of catechizing for afternoon sermons prove controversial [**4.9**]?
5 Comment on the final sentence of **4.9**.
6 'He seeketh to keep the people in darkness and blind superstition'. Do documents **4.8** and **4.9** bear out this judgement on Laud?

One major set of charges against Charles and Laud, then, concerns 'ceremonialism' – an emphasis on allegedly 'popish' or 'superstitious' practices that the Puritans had hoped to squeeze out of the Church and which were now made central to its practice. A further set of charges surround Laud's and Charles' separation of Church and State – their apparent willingness to free the Church from the interference of laymen, whether that meant the right of the common law to involve itself with Church affairs, or the rights of landowners to run the Church their own way. Document **4.10** demonstrates Laud's tough attitude towards the King's judges when they attempted to inhibit the Church courts from punishing Sir Giles Allington for ravishing and marrying (for her money) his young niece and ward. Document **4.11** is an extract from one of the annual reports on the state of the Church which Laud drew up for Charles. (The comment in the margin initialled C.R. was added by the King.) Document **4.12**, drawn from the impeachment of Laud, indicates how his enemies viewed his policies.

4.10

> If this prohibition had taken place, I hope my Lord's Grace of
> Canterbury would have excommunicated throughout his province all
> the judges who should have had a hand therein. For mine own part, I
> will assure you, if he would not I would have done it in my diocese,
> and myself in person denounced it, both in [St Paul's Cathedral] and   5
> other churches of the same, against the authors of so enormous a
> scandal to our Church and religion.

> **From Laud's speech in the Court of High Commission, 1633, in
> W. H. Hutton, *William Laud*, 1895, p. 103**

4.11

> 1637   The churchyards in many places
> are extremely annoyed and profaned,
> especially in corporate towns. And at St
> Edmundsbury the assizes are yearly kept
> in a remote side of the churchyard, and a   5
> common ale-house stands in the middle of
> the churchyard: the like abuses by ale-
> houses, back-doors, and throwing out of
> filth, with something else not fit to be
> related here, are found at Bungay: at St   10
> Mary's ad Turrim in Ipswich, at
> Woodbridge, and at Norwich, the sign-
> posts of two or three inns stand in the
> churchyard. Of remedy for these abuses,
> the bishop is utterly in despair, unless   15
> your majesty be pleased to take some

special order for them: because they which
have these back-doors into churchyards or
common passages, will plead prescription,
and then a prohibition will be granted
against the ecclesiastical proceedings.

*C.R. – Let him do his
duty, and I shall take
care, that no prohibition
shall trouble him in this* 20
case.

William Laud, Report on the state of the Church, in *The Works of
William Laud*, **vol. V, p. 351**

4.12

VI He hath traiterously assumed to himself a papal and tyrannical
power, both in Ecclesiastical and Temporal Matters, over his
majesty's subjects in this realm of England, and other places, to the
disinherison [= undermining] of the crown, dishonour of his
majesty, and derogation of his supreme authority in ecclesiastical   5
matters. And the said Archbishop claims the king's Ecclesiastical
Jurisdiction, as incident to his episcopal and archiepiscopal office in
this kingdom; and doth deny the same to be derived from the crown
of England; which he hath accordingly exercised, to the high
contempt of his royal majesty, and to the destruction of divers of the   10
king's liege people in their persons and estates . . .

**From the Impeachment Articles presented to the House of
Commons, 26 February 1641, in** *The Works of William Laud*, **vol. III,
p. 406**

Questions

1   What might many have found offensive about Laud's comments in
    4.10?
2   Why might the judges have decided (with loss of face) to back down
    over their decision to prohibit the Church courts from determining
    the Allington case [**4.10**]?
3   Comment on the phrase 'they . . . will plead prescription' [**4.11,
    lines 17–19**].
4   How might Charles I 'take care, that no prohibition shall trouble
    him.' [**4.11, lines 19–22**]?
5   Documents **4.10** and **4.11** are typical of the statements for which
    Laud was impeached [**4.12**]. Do you think that the charge in **4.12** is
    justified?

Laud was also accused of betraying the Protestant identity of the Church of England, and of seeking to realign it with the Roman Catholic Church. Document **4.13**, drawn from Laud's diary, reveals that the Pope instructed his Nuncio (papal ambassador) to offer to make Laud a Cardinal if he would effect a reconciliation of the two churches. Documents **4.14a** and **b** offer Laud's considered views of the relationship of Roman Catholicism and Protestantism and **4.15** shows the way such views were used against him in 1641.

4.13

> 1633   Aug. 17. Saturday.
> I had a serious offer made me again to be a Cardinal: I was then
> from Court, but so soon as I came thither (which was Wednesday,
> Aug. 21) I acquainted his Majesty with it. But my answer again was,   5
> that somewhat dwelt within me, which would not suffer that, till
> Rome were other than it is . . .
>
> **Extract from Laud's Diary, 1633, in** *The Works of William Laud*, **vol. III, p. 219**

4.14a

> The Protestants did not get that name by protesting against the
> Church of Rome, but by protesting (and that when nothing else
> would serve) against her errors and superstitions. Do you but remove
> them from the Church of Rome, and our Protestation is ended, and
> the separation too . . .
>
> *The Works of William Laud*, **vol. II, p. 152**

4.14b

> She professes the ancient Catholic faith, and yet the Romanist
> condemns her of novelty in her doctrine; she practises Church
> government as it hath been in use in all ages and all places where the
> Church of Christ hath taken any rooting, both in and ever since the
> Apostles' times, and yet the Separatist condemns her for anti-   5
> Christianism in her discipline. The plain truth is, she is between
> these two factions, as between two millstones, and unless your
> Majesty look to it, to whose trust she is committed, she will be

ground to powder, to an irreparable dishonour and loss to this kingdom.

William Laud, quoted in W. Hutton, *William Laud*, 1895, p. 147

4.15

VII That he [Laud] hath traitorously endeavoured to alter and subvert God's true Religion by law established in this realm; and instead thereof, to set up Popish Superstition and Idolatry; and to that end hath declared and maintained in Speeches and printed Books divers Popish Doctrines and Opinions, contrary to the Articles of   5
Religion established by law. He hath urged and enjoined divers popish and superstitious ceremonies, without any warrant of law; and hath cruelly persecuted those who have opposed the same, by corporal punishment and imprisonment; and most unjustly vexed others who refused to conform thereto, by Ecclesiastical Censures of   10
Excommunication, Suspension, Deprivation, and Degradation, contrary to the law of the kingdom . . .

X He hath traitorously and wickedly endeavoured to reconcile the Church of England with the Church of Rome . . .

Impeachment Articles, in *The Works of William Laud*, vol. III, pp. 407, 411

Questions

1 Comment on the *tone* of **4.13**. When Laud's prosecutors read his diary in 1641, they thought this entry supported the charge in **4.15**, lines **13–14**. Is that fair?

2 Do **4.14a** and **b** constitute evidence for **4.15**?

3 How would Puritans have described the position of the Church of England in relation to (i) Rome   (ii) Geneva?

Laud's opponents included people who believed that he was departing from the mainstream of Elizabethan and Jacobean Protestantism, and who hoped to return to that tradition. Of those opponents, some, maybe reacting against his policies, became ever more convinced that England needed a second reformation – the abolition of bishops and existing forms of worship, and the introduction of Church government and practice closely modelled on the 'best reformed churches' abroad. Document **4.16** is an extract from one of the most savage attacks on Laud and his fellow-bishops, and **4.17** tells what happened to the authors as a result.

4.16

Now I beseech you look upon the pride and ingratitude of [the
bishops]. What is it that this world can yield unto mortal creatures,
that they possess not? Great and mighty are their privileges, and yet
they are neither thankful to God nor the King . . . but would have
more. They have the keys of heaven to shut out whom they will.   5
They have the keys of hell, to thrust in whom they please. They have
the keys also of our purses to pick them at their pleasure . . . They
have the keys likewise of all the prisons in the kingdom . . .
    But how magnificent and glorious will [Laud] be . . . having . . . a
great number of gentlemen . . . waiting on him; some of them   10
carrying up his tail, for the better breaking and venting of his wind
. . . when he goeth in state and in great power to Cambridge and
Oxford in his metropolitical rogation and perambulation, and with a
rod in his hand . . . to whip those naughty scholars, that will not
learn well their lessons of conformity . . . nor will not cringe to the 15
altar, nor turn their faces to the East, nor worship the communion
table . . . For the Church is now as full of ceremonies, as a dog is full
of fleas . . .

The Letany of John Bastwick, 1637, pp. 4–6, 17

4.17

[John Bastwick, Henry Burton and William Prynne were summoned
before the Star Chamber] for writing and publishing seditious,
schismatical and libellous books against the Hierarchy . . . Dr
Bastwick . . . termed the Prelates invaders of the King's Prerogative
. . . advancers of popery, superstition, idolatry, profaneness,   5
oppression of the King's subjects, enemies of God and the King, and
servants of the Devil . . .
    The Court . . . fined the three . . . £5,000 apiece to the King . . .
to stand in the pillory . . . Bastwick and Burton to lose their ears, and
Prynne the remainder of his ears; Prynne to be stigmatised on both   10
cheeks with the letters S.L. signifying a seditious libeller: all of them
to suffer perpetual imprisonment . . .

J. Rushworth, *Historical Collections*, 1659, vol. II, pp. 273, 283, 293–5

Questions

1   What were Bastwick's objections to the bishops [4.16], and why do you think the Church authorities would disapprove of his pamphlet?
2   Is there any indication that Rushworth's account [4.17] is biased?
3   Consider how severe the sentences were by the standard of the time.
4   This was one of only a handful of such trials and punishments. Can this policy of striking terror by making examples of a few be justified?

Finally, we can sum up the charges brought against the Church under Charles and Laud. Here is the measured prose of John Pym [4.18] and the intemperate prose of an Essex gentleman called Harbottle Grimston [4.19].

4.18

There are A Threefold sort of Grievances: 1. Some against the Privilege of Parliament. 2. Others to the prejudice of Religion. 3. Some against the Liberty of the Subject . . .

The second is, Encouragement of Popery: First, By Suspension of Laws against them: Now 'tis certain, there can be no Security from   5
Papists, but in their Disability; Their Principles are incompatible with any other Religion; Laws will not restrain them, nor Oaths; for the Pope dispenseth with both . . . 2. By allowing them Places of Trust and Honour in the Commonwealth. 3. Their Free Resort to London . . . 4. . . . have they a Nuncio here . . .   10

Then as to Innovations of Religion introduced: First, Maintenance of Popish Tenets, in Books, Sermons, and Disputations. 2. Practice of Popish Ceremonies countenanced and enjoined, as Altars, Images, Crucifixes, Bowings, &c. These I may in some respect compare to the Dry Bones in Ezekiel; which first came together, then Sinews and   15
Flesh came upon them, afterwards the Skin cover'd them, and then Breath and Life was put into them; so first the Form, then the Spirit, and Life of Popery was to come amongst us. 3. Preferment of Persons Popishly affected. 4. The discouragement of Protestants by over-rigid Prosecutions of the scrupulous for things indifferent: No Vice made   20
so great as Inconformity; by Punishing without Law, for not Reading the Book for Sunday Recreations; for not removing the Communion Table otherwise; for not coming to the Rails to receive the Communion; for Preaching on the Lords Day if the Afternoon . . . 5. By incroachment of Ecclesiastical Jurisdiction . . .

John Pym in J. Rushworth, *Historical Collections*, vol. III, p. 30.

4.19

Mr Speaker, we are now fallen upon the great Man the Arch-Bishop
of Canterbury; look upon him as he is in Highness, and he is the Sty
of all Pestilential filth, that hath infested the State and Government
of this Commonwealth: Look upon him in his dependencies, and he
is the only Man, the only Man that hath raised and advanced all   5
those, that together with himself, have been the Authors and Causers
of all our Ruines, Miseries, and Calamities we now groan under . . .

Who is it, Mr Speaker, but he only, that hath advanced all our
Popish Bishops? . . . These are the men that should have fed Christ's
Flock, but they are the Wolves that have devoured them; the Sheep   10
should have fed upon the Mountains, but the Mountains have eaten
up the Sheep . . .

Who is it, Mr Speaker, but this great Arch-Bishop of Canterbury,
that hath sat at the Helm, to steer, and manage all the Projects that
have been set on foot in this Kingdom . . .? There is scarce any   15
Grievance, or Complaint come before us in this place, wherein we do
not find him intermentioned, and as it were twisted into it, like a
busy, angry Wasp, his Sting is in the tail of every thing . . .

Mr Speaker, he hath been the great and Common Enemy of all
Goodness, and Good men; and it is not safe that such a Viper should   20
be near His Majesty's Person, to distil his Poison into His Sacred
Ears.

**Speech by Harbottle Grimston in the House of Commons, 8
November 1640, in J. Rushworth, *Historical Collections*, vol. III, p. 30**

Questions

1   Look at Pym's allegations [4.18]. How many of them are borne out
    by the evidence you have seen?
2   Draft Laud's defence against *two* of the charges in **4.18**.
3   Those who believed that Laud was guilty of those charges believed
    that he should be executed, and he was indeed beheaded for them.
    Why did they think the charges were so serious?
4   Comment on the *tone* of **4.19**.
5   Do you find it surprising that no-one rebuked or criticized Grimston
    for his speech?

5 Personal Rule 1629–40

The period between the dissolution of Charles I's third Parliament in 1629 and the summoning of the Short Parliament in 1640 is usually known as the 'Personal Rule'. This term is intended to sum up two separate aspects of the period: that Charles I was his own first minister; and that he governed through institutions and officials personally chosen by and answerable to him, rather than in co-operation with representatives of the 'estates of the realm' gathered in Parliament.

After the death of Buckingham, Charles had no favourites. There were several influential ministers – notably Archbishop Laud and Lord Treasurer Weston. But no-one who carried the authority (or the responsibility) that Lord Burghley and his son Robert Cecil, Earl of Salisbury, had carried for the fifty years from 1558 to 1612, or who commanded the power and personal hold over the monarch that Buckingham possessed throughout the 1620s. The dominant personality of the 1630s, Thomas Wentworth, (created Earl of Strafford in 1640), spent the decade away from the centre of power (governing first the North of England and then Ireland), and there is no evidence that Charles *liked* him. Observers close to the Court were aware that the person closest to the King was his French Catholic Queen, Henrietta-Maria, and (in the later 1630s), the man whose company he most enjoyed was George Con, the papal envoy. (For the fears this unleashed, see Chapter 6.)

Charles' Personal Rule was not a period of drift. Charles saw it as years of refurbishment and reform: departments of State were to be made more efficient, all office-holders were required to carry out their appointed duties; the central government would lay down much clearer guidelines, and expected regular reports from local officials. The 'Book of Orders', issued in 1631, streamlined Poor Law administration; the Judges were issued with clear instructions which they were to pass on to local magistrates in long addresses as they toured the country on assize circuit. Close attention was paid to improving the training and equipment of the militia. Historians differ about how effective all this was. 'A drive for unity through uniformity,' one historian called it. Some feel that the imposition of nationally conceived and rigidly imposed schemes made many local governors unco-operative – but these were not years of drift.

Furthermore the return to peace brought a return to stable finances. Charles' drive to increase his revenue caused resentment and protest, but he did balance the budget and reduce levels of royal indebtedness (we should remember that princes all over Europe were increasing taxes at this time without provoking revolution). By 1637 Charles' revenue was over £1 million – in real terms double the income James had inherited in 1603, and fifty per cent higher than Charles' income had been in 1625. Only one source of income – Ship Money – was causing even passive resistance, and that was largely ineffectual.

Many historians have assumed that the failure of the Personal Rule was inevitable, but contemporaries clearly did not think so. There was no increase in levels of public violence; fewer treason and sedition trials than in any decade for which records survive; no boycott or collapse of the courts or of local government. England was not sliding into chaos and anarchy.

Many people wrote in their memoirs about the 1630s as 'halcyon' days of peace and prosperity: but such views were written *after* the traumas and nightmares of civil war. Less easy to dismiss are the views typified by documents **5.1** and **5.2**, recorded at the time. Document **5.1** was written by a Cambridge don who provided a regular news service for those living abroad or remote from London. This is from a report sent to Charles' ambassador in Paris. Document **5.2** is from a review of the state of England written in 1633.

5.1

All things are at this instant here in that calmness that there is very little matter of novelty to write, for there appears no change or alteration either in court or affairs, for all business goes undisturbedly on in the strong current of the present time to which all men for the most part submit, and that effects this quietness. And although   5
payments here are great (considering the people have not heretofore been accustomed unto them) yet they only privately breathe out a little discontented humour and lay down their purses, for I think that great tax of the ship money is so well digested (the honour of the business sinking now into apprehension and amongst most winning   10
an affection to it) I suppose will become perpetual; for indeed if men would consider the great levies of monies in foreign parts for the service of the state, these impositions would appear but little burdens, but time can season and form minds to comply with public necessities.

John Burghe to Viscount Scudamore, October 1637, from Public Record Office, C115/N4/861

5.2

> We know not what a Rebel is; what a Plotter against the
> Commonwealth: nor what that is, which Grammarians call Treason:
> the names themselves are antiquated with the Things.
>
> **Sir Henry Wootton, 'Panegyrick to Charles I', 1633, in** *Reliquiae*
> *Wottonianae*, **4th edn, 1683, p. 151**

Keep an open mind about these documents as you read through the
chapter. There are questions about them at the end (page 90).

Charles wished to bring order wherever there was chaos or disorganiza-
tion. Documents **5.3a** and **b** and **5.4** are typical of the stream of proclamations that he issued in the 1630s. Both should be self-explanatory.
Document **5.5** brings us to murkier matters. Charles, like his predecessors,
created monopolies – granting to individuals or groups the sole right to
manufacture or to market specified goods. Much of this had always been
uncontroversial – protecting domestic goods from foreign competition,
protecting inventors from being taken advantage of, ensuring quality
control etc. But a minority of monopolies had always been controversial,
especially since the 1590s. The grant of monopoly could be, and often was,
more designed to give courtiers and others control of a lucrative market,
with profits swollen by the grant of monopoly – profits which the Crown
could share. Such monopolies benefited the Exchequer rather than the
economy. Documents **5.5** and **5.6a** and **b** make the case for and against one
of the many controversial monopolies created in the 1630s.

5.3a

> Whereas by the grace and blessing of God, the Kings and Queens of
> this Realm, by many ages past, have had the happiness, by their
> sacred touch and invocation of the name of God, to cure those who
> are afflicted with the disease called the King's Evil:[1] And his now
> Majesty, in no less measure than any of His Royal Predecessors, hath   5
> had good success therein: and in His most gracious and pious
> disposition, is as ready and willing as any King or Queen of this
> Realm ever was, in any thing to relieve the distresses and necessities
> of His Subjects. Yet in His Princely wisdom, foreseeing that in this,
> (as in all other things) Order is to be observed, and fit times are   10
> necessary to be appointed for performing of this great work of
> charity; His most Excellent Majesty doth hereby publish and declare

His Royal Will and Pleasure to be, That whereas heretofore the usual times of presenting such persons to His Majesty for this purpose, were Easter and Whitsuntide, That from henceforth the times shall   15 be Easter and Michaelmas, as times more convenient, both for the temperature of the season, and in respect of any contagion which may happen in this near access to His Majesty's sacred Person . . . And His Majesty doth further Will . . . That all such . . . shall bring with them Certificates under the hands of the Parson, Vicar or Minister,   20 and Churchwardens . . . and under the hands and seals of one or more Justices of the Peace for . . . testifying . . . That they have not at any time before been touched by the King, to the intent to be healed of that Disease.

¹ also known as 'scrofula' – a chronic swelling of the glands

Royal Proclamation, 28 July 1635, in J. F. Larkin (ed.), *Stuart Royal Proclamations, II, King Charles I, 1625–46,* **1983, pp. 466–7**

5.3b

His Majesty understanding that by the liberty now taken to keep greyhounds about his Court, and in the places adjoining, the game of hares is destroyed, where they ought to be preserved for his royal desport, doth thereupon strictly inhibit and forbid as well the followers of his Court as other gentlemen, and all persons of what   5 quality soever, to keep or suffer to be kept any greyhounds or mongrels within ten miles where his Court shall reside. And withal commandeth all his gamekeepers . . . diligently to search and enquire for all such greyhounds and mongrels . . . and to seize the same, and cause them to be presently put away, hanged up, or otherwise   10 destroyed.

Royal Proclamation, 4 March 1638, in J. F. Larkin (ed.), *Stuart Royal Proclamations, II, King Charles I, 1625–46,* **1983, p. 598**

5.4

The king's most excellent Majesty hath observed that of late years a great number of the nobility and gentry, and abler sort of his people, with their families, have resorted to the cities of London and Westminster, and places adjoining, and there made their residence

more than in former times, contrary to the ancient usage of the   5
English nation . . . For where[as] by their residence and abiding in
the several counties where their means ariseth, they served the king
in several places according to their degree and ranks, in aid of the
government, whereby, and by their housekeeping in those parts, the
realm was defended and the meaner sort of people were guided,   10
directed and relieved; but by their residence in the said cities . . .
they have not employment, but live without doing any service to his
Majesty or his people, a great part of their money and substance is
drawn from the several counties whence it ariseth, and is spent in the
city in excess of apparel provided from foreign parts, to the enriching   15
of other nations and unnecessary consumption of a great part of the
treasure of this realm, and in other delights and expenses, even to the
wasting of their estates, which is not issued into the parts whence it
ariseth, nor are the people of them relieved therewith or by their
hospitality, nor yet set on work, as they might and would be . . . also   20
the prices of all kinds of victuals . . . are exceedingly increased . . .

   Therefore his Majesty doth straitly charge and command . . . [the
nobility and gentry to] depart from the cities of London and
Westminster . . . and resort to the several counties where they usually
resided . . . upon such pains as are to be inflicted upon those that   25
shall neglect the public service and defence of the realm, in contempt
of his Majesty's royal command.

Royal Proclamation, 20 June 1632, in J. P. Kenyon (ed.), *The Stuart
Constitution 1603–1688: Documents and Commentary*, 2nd edn, 1986,
pp. 455–6

5.5

Well weighing . . . that this Our Kingdom is endowed by God's
blessing with many natural and useful Materials, for the employment
and setting on work the Natives and People thereof, who are now
grown to be very numerous and populous, and many of them poor
for want of means of employment;   5
   And some years past We have received Information, that Pot-ashes
and Soap-ashes, wherewith Soap was usually made, were by the
charge, invention, and industry of divers of Our Subjects, made of
Materials of Our own Kingdom . . . And We having likewise received
information that as good, sweet, and useful Soap as ever had been   10

formerly made, was made of the same Pot-ashes and other Materials
of Our own Dominions, whereby the Treasure of Our Kingdom
might be preserved from employment of Strangers, and Our own
Subjects thereby relieved and set on work at home. We . . . did
desire to give all encouragement and assistance to a Work of so much   15
advantage and benefit to this Kingdom and people, yet withall took
care to be fully and clearly satisfied, that Our loving Subjects in
general might not in any wise be thereby abused or deceived,
whereupon by advice and order of the Lords and others of our Privy
Council, Sir Robert Ducie . . . then Lord Mayor of our City of   20
London, was required to make trial of the Soap . . . with the best
Soap formerly used . . . and thereupon certified that he found that
the Soap made with the Pot-ashes and Materials of Our own
Dominions, did wash both whiter and sweeter . . .

Whereupon We being desirous to give all just encouragements to a   25
Work so beneficial for Our people . . . did grant to divers of our
Subjects privilege for the term of fourteen years, for the making of
hard and soft Soap, with such materials, as had been by them newly
invented . . . We did carefully provide that the said Corporation
should furnish this Kingdom with sufficient quantities of good and   30
sweet Soap, And that they should sell the same at, and for reasonable
prices, not exceeding three pence the pound . . .

And We did thereby prohibit that none should put to sale any
Soap or other the premises, before such time as the Searchers or their
Deputies, the same were viewed and found to be sweet and well   35
made, and by them marked with the mark appointed for that
purpose.

Royal Proclamation, 26 January 1634, in J. F. Larkin (ed.), *Stuart*
Royal Proclamations, II, King Charles I, 1625–46, **1983, pp. 396–8**

5.6a

Many citizens of London were put out of an old Trade, in which
they had been bred all their time, and which was their only
livelihood, by knights and esquires and gentlemen, never bred up to
the Trade, upon pretence of a Project and new Invention, which in
truth was not so, their prosecution of the soapmakers of London in   5
Star Chamber, being beyond example, both in respect of the manner
of their proceedings, and of the sentence itself, who for using fish oil,

and not obeying their searchers, were fined at great sums, imprisoned
at three several times about twenty months, their goods extended,
their pans, vats etcs broken and destroyed, their houses   10
[= households] dispersed and necessitated; and their estates almost
ruined.

A True Relation of the State of the Business Concerning Soap, 1641

5.6b

It is indeed all too true that some, or rather many, especially amongst
the Jesuits and Benedictines, have turned to dealing in stocks rather
than in souls; and in particular it is said of Basil [= Sir Basil Brooke,
one of the patentees] and his partner that he entered the new soap
business with Jesuit backing. The new soap is, because of the   5
peoples' dislike of it and because its origins is [*sic*] known, called
Popish Soap.

**Gregorio Panzani, papal agent in England to the Pope, February
1635; translation from the Italian as printed in S. R. Gardiner,**
History of England . . . 1603–42, **vol. VIII, p. 74, note 1**

Questions

1   In what ways do **5.3a** and **b** and **5.4** illuminate Charles I's conception
     of government?
2   Why might the gentry have preferred life in London to life in the
     country [**5.4**]?
3   How reasonable do you think Charles I's command is in **5.4**?
4   Does **5.6a** show the argument of **5.5** to be specious?
5   Those who were granted the soap monopoly were Catholic members
     of the Queen's entourage. Does this affect your assessment of
     document **5.5**?
6   The Stuart Monarchs were the last English dynasty to touch for the
     King's Evil. What was the significance of this ceremony – included in
     the Prayer book in 1634 – and why do you think Charles I employed
     it so frequently?

The success of Charles' financial policies in the 1630s rested upon tighter
control of expenditure and the maximizing of revenues. This included the
ruthless development of Crown lands (through enclosure, etc.); and en-
hancements of impositions (surcharges on customs, the source of much

controversy in Parliament since 1610). There was also a recourse to 'fiscal feudalism' – the resurrection of long-existing but largely forgotten rights, such as the right to levy fines on those who encroached into ancient royal forest, and the right to levy fines on those possessing freehold land yielding £40 per year who did not take up knighthoods at the time of the King's coronation. Such devices were surprisingly lucrative and little resisted. By far the most controversial of the revenue devices of the 1630s, however, was Ship Money. The King claimed the right to levy rates in a national emergency to equip a fleet in defence of the realm. This had regularly been claimed by Charles' predecessors, but once a generation. From 1634 to 1639 Charles demanded it every year, and, controversially if not unprecedently, levied it not just on coastal regions, but across the nation. The sums involved (far more per annum than any parliamentary grant), and the extension of the duty to pay many not-hitherto-required national taxes, added to the controversy. The following documents [5.7–5.13] look at the controversy surrounding Ship Money. Document **5.7** comes from one of the writs issued by Charles; **5.8** and **5.9** come from the Judges' decisions when the legality of Ship Money was tested in Court – a case the King won by a large majority; document **5.10** shows some of the problems sheriffs faced in levying the rate, and **5.11** offers unique insight into a discussion amongst provincial gentry about the issues raised by Ship Money. Document **5.12** is the later judgement of the Earl of Clarendon on the damage Charles did himself through this policy. Remember that although Clarendon was a severe critic of the Personal Rule at the time, by the time he wrote his history he was a principal adviser of the monarchy. Document **5.13** indicates how some of the money was spent!

5.7

To the Sheriff of our County of Bucks . . . Greeting. Because it is given to us to understand that Certain Thieves pirates & Robbers at sea, As well Enemies to the name of Christ, as other Mahomitans having gathered together ships and the goods and Merchandise not only of our subjects, but also of the subjects of our friends at sea,   5
which by the English people in times past used to be defended, wickedly taking away and spoiling them at their pleasure, have carried away, And the men in the same into miserable captivity taking . . . Considering also the dangers which on every side these warlike times do threaten, so that it behoveth us and our subjects to   10
hasten the defence of the sea and Kingdom with all speed, We willing the defence of our kingdom . . . the security of our subjects, the safe

conduct of our ships, and Merchandise . . . we command that one
Ship of War of the burden of four hundred and fifty ton, with men
. . . an Hundred and four score at the least, and also Guns . . . and   15
other Arms necessary . . . and also with victual, until the first day of
March next following, for so many men fit, And from that time for
twenty-six weeks, at your costs as well in victuals, as mens' wages,
and other necessaries for war during that time for the defence of the
sea . . . We have assigned you . . . to make such Assessments upon   20
the . . . Boroughs & parishes [of Buckinghamshire], and members of
them, as you shall see reasonable to be done.

**Ship Money Writ, issued by Charles I, 1635, in C. G. Bousey and
J. G. Jenkins (eds.), 'Ship Money Papers', *Buckinghamshire Record
Society*, vol. XIII, 1975, pp. 1–2**

5.8

Where Mr Holborne [one of Hampden's lawyers] supposed a
fundamental policy in the creation of the frame of this kingdom, that
in case the monarch of England should be inclined to exact from his
subjects at his pleasure, he should be restrained, for that he could
have nothing from them, but upon a common consent in Parliament.   5
   He is utterly mistaken herein. I agree the Parliament to be a most
ancient and supreme court, where the King and Peers, as judges, are
in person, and the whole body of the Commons representatively . . .
   But the former fancied policy I utterly deny. The law knows no
such king-yoking policy. The law is of itself an old and trusty servant 10
of the King's; it is his instrument or means which he useth to govern
his people by . . .
   Though I have gone already very high, I shall go yet to a higher
contemplation of the fundamental policy of our laws: which is this,
that the King of mere right ought to have, and the people of mere   15
duty are bound to yield unto the King, supply for the defence of the
kingdom. And when the Parliament itself doth grant supply in that
case, it is not merely a benevolence of the people, but therein they do
an act of justice and duty to the King.

**Sir Robert Berkeley, Justice of the King's Bench, 1638, in S. R.
Gardiner, *Constitutional Documents of the Puritan Revolution*, 1906,
pp. 114–15, 121–3**

5.9

This is a case of as great consequence as ever came judicially into any
Court, therefore it behoveth us to be as careful in delivering
judgement in it . . . To show that judgement ought not to be given
against Mr Hampden, I shall deliver my reasons, which shall stand
upon these po[sitions].   5

1 That the writ of 4th August directed to the sheriff of Bucks to
provide a ship, with munition, etc, at the charge of the inhabitants of
the county and to rate them, etc, is against the common law, for that
is not by assent in Parliament.

2 That it is against divers statutes.   10

3 That no pretence of prerogative, royal power, necessity, or
danger, doth or can make it good.

4 That it is not warranted by any precedents vouched, especially
not by any one record judicial; but rather in my understanding
express records against the legality of these writs . . .   15

5 That the motives of the writ are not sufficient to lay this charge
upon the county, and are not warranted by former precedents.

6 If they were, yet the command of the writ is against the law.

7 If the writ were legal, yet the manner of assessment by the
sheriff as it is certified is not warranted by the writ . . .   20

We are not to judge here according to conveniency or state policy,
but according to the common law and custom of England we are to
judge. We find in our books, records or statutes; if we cannot find it
to be law by these we cannot judge it to be law . . .

The common law of England sets a freedom in the subjects in   25
respect of their persons, and gives them a true property in their
goods and estates; so that without their consent (that is to say their
private actual consent or implicity in Parliament) it cannot be taken
from them. And as to this purpose the law distinguishes between
bondmen, whose estates are at their lords' will and disposition, and   30
freemen, whose property none may invade; for in our case here is a
charge laid upon the free subject without his consent, and therefore
not warranted by the law.

Sir George Croke, Justice of the King's Bench, quoted in W. J. Jones,
Politics and the Bench, **1971, pp. 186–8**

5.10

Mr Sheriff hath a little suspended the full execution of this service
in respect of many oppositions made, which until these Doubts are
resolved by your Lordships he knows not how to persist in the
service between he fears one opposition may draw on another to the
prejudice of the service which he would avoid . . .   5

To know . . . whether a Hamlet that lies in some other Country
than Buck[ingham]shire shall pay with the Parish that lies in
Buck[ingham]shire and ever paid with the Parish in Buck[ingham]-
shire & never in the County of Oxford, nor doth not of itself, nor
with any other Town pay . . .   10

To have directions how to divide the Sums into Hundreds and
Parishes I do find that some Hundred hath a Hamlet lies in it and
belongs to a Parish in another Hundred what to do in that case . . .

Whether I shall alter the Rates that be set by the Assessors in
every Parish concerning the rich men or to let them go as they be   15
assessed by the Assessors, for if I should not raise them I know not
how to relieve the poorer sort according to his Majesty's desire . . .

Whether shall the Sheriff distrain, for he is threatened to be sued,
if he do. And if he do distrain what shall he do with the cattle.

C. G. Bousey and J. G. Jenkins (eds.), 'Ship Money Papers',
Buckinghamshire Record Society, **vol. XIII, 1975, pp. 8–10**

5.11

At the assizes at Maidstone, Judge Weston . . . acquainted the
country with this question . . . from the king and the judges' answer
to it . . . but when he came to speak of ship-money, the audience
which had before hearkened but with ordinary attention did then (as
to that did nigh concern them) listen with great diligence, and after   5
the declaration made I did, in my conceit, see a kind of dejection in
their very looks . . .

Some held my lord keeper's speech very moderate, that more could
not be hoped for from a prince then in causes of weight to proceed
by the advice of his judges and that the declaration the judges had   10
made was fully to the point and by that the king had full right to
impose it, and all concluded that if a kingdom were in jeopardy it
ought not [to] be lost for want of money if it were within it, which

these men said we were to believe the king affirming, and that it was
a great grace and favour that he would not deny any his lawful trial.   15

Others argued far differingly that it could not but be expected that
a just king would take counsel of his judges in a case of this weight,
the greatest was ever heard at a common bar in England, that in a
judgment that not may but doth touch every man in so high a point
every man ought to be heard . . . They confessed the last parliaments 20
had been much to blame in their carriages towards his majesty, but
the goodness of monarchs had formerly forgot as great errors . . .

Sir Edward Littleton Mr Solicitor's speech did not pass without
censure, many wondering what that record by him mentioned in
Edward I his time should be . . .   25

No man will doubt but these thoughts and many more past in
men's minds that shall understand this was the greatest cause
according to the general opinion of the world was ever heard out of
parliament in England. And the common sort of people are sensible
of no loss of liberty so much as that hath joined with it a parting   30
from money . . .

Whether this way of taxing the country were like to continue . . .

To the first many were persuaded this way would not last to raise
money by. They did observe that new laws did rather lose their own
credit than abolish that which time, use, and approbation had   35
contributed to old. That the introducing a new way in any business
had no greater enemy than the many inconveniences might arise by
putting it in execution. That this was full of many such, by giving
the High Sheriff an unlimited power, from whom there was no
appeal but the council board, so full of trouble.

**Memorandum in the Papers of Sir Roger Twysden, a JP in Kent,
Kent Archives Office, ed. Kenneth Fincham in *The Bulletin of the
Institute of Historical Research*, vol. LVII, no. 136, 1984, pp. 232–5**

5.12

And here the damage and mischief cannot be expressed, that the
Crown and State sustained by the deserved reproach and infamy that
attended the judges, by being made use of in this and like acts of
power; there being no possibility to preserve the dignity, reverence
and estimation of the laws themselves but by the integrity and   5
innocency of the judges. And no question, as the exorbitancy of the

House of Commons this parliament hath proceeded principally from their contempt of laws, and that contempt from the scandal of that judgment . . . who had always before looked upon [the judges] as the oracles of the law, and the best guides and directors of their opinions 10 and actions: and they now thought themselves excused for swerving from the rules and customs of their predecessors (who in altering and making of laws . . . had always observed the advice and judgement of those sages) in not asking questions of those whom they knew nobody would believe . . . If [the judges] had preserved the simplicity of their 15 ancestors in severely and strictly defending the laws, other men had observed the modesty of theirs in humbly and dutifully obeying them.

Edward Hyde, Earl of Clarendon, *The History of the Rebellion and Civil Wars in England begun in the year 1641,* **W. D. Macray (ed.), 1888, vol. I, p. 124**

5.13

The Sovereign of the Seas

How forward and indulgent his sacred Majesty hath been, and still is, not only in the repairing, but increasing his Royal Navy above all the Princes that have preceded him . . .

I began at the beak-head, where . . . there is a Cupid, or a child 5 resembling him, bestriding and bridling a Lion, which importeth, that sufferance may curb insolence, and innocency restrain violence; which alludeth to the great mercy of the King, whose type is a proper emblem of that great Majesty, whose Mercy is above all his Works . . . 10

There are other things in this Vessel worthy remark, at least, if not admiration; namely, that one Tree, or Oak made of some of the principal beams of this great ship, which was forty-four foot of strong and serviceable timber in length, three foot diameter at the top, and ten foot diameter at the stub or bottom . . . She hath two galleries of 15 a side, and all of most curious carved work, and all the sides of the ship are carved also with trophies . . . gilded quite over, and no other colour but gold and black to be seen about her . . . Her length by the keel is 128 foot or thereabout . . . Her main breadth . . . 48 foot . . . She is in height . . . seventy-six foot . . . She hath three flush decks, 20 and a forecastle, a half deck, a quarterdeck, and a round-house. Her

lower tier hath thirty ports, which are to be furnished with demi-cannon and whole cannon throughout . . . Her middle tier hath also thirty ports for demi-culverin, and whole culverin: Her third tier hath twenty-six ports for other ordnance, her forecastle hath twelve ports,   25
and her half deck hath fourteen ports. She hath thirteen or fourteen ports more within board for murdering pieces, besides a great many loopholes out of the cabins for musket shot . . . which considered together, seeing his Majesty is at this infinite charge, both for the honour of this Nation, and the security of his Kingdom, it should be   30
a great spur and encouragement to all his faithful and loving subjects to be liberal and willing contributaries towards the Ship Money . . .

Captain Phineas Pett [is] Overseer of the work, and . . . the Master Builder is young M. Peter Pett, who before he was full five and twenty years of age, made the Model, and since hath perfected the   35
work.

A True description of his majesty's Royal Ship, 1637

Questions

1   Summarize the case for the collection of Ship Money, as laid out in documents **5.7**, **5.8** and **5.11**.
2   Summarize the case against the collection of Ship Money, as laid out in documents **5.9**, **5.10**, and **5.11**.
3   More than 90 per cent (ie. at least £$\frac{3}{4}$ million) of all Ship Money demanded between 1634 and 1638 was collected. Does this demonstrate the strength of the Personal Rule?
4   Documents **5.10** and **5.11** illustrate the problems faced by those who had to assess and collect Ship Money. Does it suggest that the collapse of co-operation in 1639–40 was the result not 'of the great constitutional issues raised by Hampden's lawyers, but a growing fear of the consequences of Ship Money for the economic and social stability of each county'?
5   Does document **5.13** suggest that the Ship Money rate was used properly, or that too much was spent on large vessels mainly for show? If Charles I was a benefactor of the Navy, why did it fail to support him in the civil war?
6   How far are you willing to place weight on document **5.12**, given that it was written many years later?
7   'The Personal Rule rested on the letter of the law, but defied the spirit of the law.' Do documents **5.7–5.12** bear this out?

In 1637 there was no reason to think that Charles' Personal Rule was in danger of collapse. But then he blundered into a confrontation with his Scottish subjects. He had only visited his Northern kingdom once (in 1633); he had systematically reduced the power of the Scottish Privy Council in Edinburgh and had governed with the advice of a small group of Scots living in London; he had threatened to cancel all the grants of Church lands made to the nobility and lairds (= gentry) after the Scottish Reformation (but had backed off as the protests grew). Above all, he had set out to bring the Scottish Church in line with the English Church. In Scotland the Reformation had been more thoroughly 'Protestant' than in England. For example, bishops, initially abandoned in Scotland, had been restored, but with an advisory rather than an executive role. No set form of liturgy had been introduced in Scotland, and worship centred around bible-reading, improvised prayer and long sermons. Charles both sought to restore the authority of the bishops and to introduce a Prayer Book which enshrined much that was characteristic of Laudian piety. Rioting greeted the new services and disaffection quickly spread to the nobility. Charles' uncompromising demands for the introduction of the Prayer Book and punishment of rioters led to the National Covenant in 1638, a solemn oath by which the greater part of all influential groups in Scotland bound themselves to resist innovation in Church and State. The deferential language of the Covenant [5.14] can be compared with the private glosses of some of its adherents [5.15]. The intransigence of the Covenanters was matched by the intransigence of the King [5.16–5.19]. The result was war.

5.14

In obedience to the Commandment of God, conform to the practice of the godly in former times, and according to the laudable example of our Worthy and Religious Progenitors, & of many yet living amongst us, which was warranted also by act of Council, commanding a general band to be made and subscribed by his   5 Majesty's subjects, of all ranks, for two causes: One was, For defending the true Religion, as it was then reformed, and is expressed in the Confession of Faith . . . The other cause was, for maintaining the King's Majesty, His Person, and Estate: the true worship of God and the King's authority, being so straitly joined, as that they did   10 stand and fall together . . . We Noblemen, Barons, Gentlemen, Burgesses, Ministers & Commons under subscribing, considering divers times before & especially at this time, the danger of the true reformed Religion, of the King's honour, and of the public peace of

the Kingdom: By the manifold innovations and evils generally   15
contained, and particularly mentioned in our late supplications,
complaints, and protestations, Do hereby profess, and before God,
his Angels, and the World solemnly declare. That, with our whole
hearts we agree & resolve, all the days of our life, constantly to
adhere unto, and to defend the foresaid true Religion, and (forbearing   20
the practice of all [in]novations, already introduced in the matters of
the worship of God, or approbation of the corruptions of the public
Government of the Kirk, or civil places and power of Kirk-men, till
they be tried & allowed in free assemblies, and in Parliaments) to
labour by all means lawful to recover the purity and liberty of the   25
Gospel, as it was stablished and professed before the foresaid
[In]novations . . . We promise and swear that we shall, to the
uttermost of our power, with our means and lives, stand to the
defence of our dread Sovereign, the King's Majesty, his Person, and
Authority, in the defence and preservation of the foresaid true   30
Religion, Liberties and Laws of the Kingdom: As also to the mutual
defence and assistance, every one of us of another in the same cause
of maintaining the true Religion and his Majesty's Authority.

**The National Covenant, February 1638, in W. C. Dickinson and G.
Donaldson, *A Source Book of Scottish History*, vol. III, (1567–1707),
1956, pp. 100–102**

5.15

The Lord has led us hitherto by the hand from step to step; and, at
every step we would have stood at, made our adversaries to refuse,
and forced us to go up a new step of reformation; so even yet in this
business he will not suffer any manner of composition or
condiscendence till he bring us to the highest step of reformation;   5
and, instead of those cautions and limitations of prelates now
contained in our articles, suffer us not to settle till we speak plain
truth according to the will of God, that is the utter overthrow and
ruin of Episcopacy, that great grandmother of all our corruptions,
[in]novations, usurpations, diseases and troubles.

**Diary of Archibald Johnston of Wariston for 4 May 1638, quoted in
W. C. Dickinson and G. Donaldson, *A Source Book of Scottish
History*, vol. III, 1956, pp. 104–5**

There now follows a sequence of extracts from four letters from Charles I to the Marquess of Hamilton, his chief negotiator with the Covenanters:

5.16

Your care must be how to dissolve the multitude; and, if it be possible, to possess yourself of my castles of Edinburgh and Stirling (which I do not expect) and to this end, I give you leave to flatter them with what hopes you please, so you engage not me against my grounds (and, in particular, that you consent neither to the calling of 5 Parliament nor General Assembly, until the Covenant be disavowed and given up). Your chief end being now to win time, that they may not commit public follies, until I be ready to suppress them. And that it is (as you well observe) my own people, which by this means will be for a time ruined; so that the loss must be inevitably mine; 10 and this if I could eschew (were it not with a greater) were well. But, when I consider that not only now my crown, but my reputation for ever, lies at stake, I must rather suffer the first that time will help, than this last, which is irreparable.

This I have written to no other end than to show you that I will 15 rather die than yield to these impertinent and damnable demands (as you rightly call them), for it is all one, as to yield to be no King in a very short time.

Charles I to Hamilton, 11 June 1638, in C. Petrie, *The Letters of King Charles I*, 1934, pp. 106–7

5.17

I shall take your advice in staying the public preparations for force; but in a silent way (by your leave) I will not leave to prepare, that I may be ready upon the least advertisement. Now, I hope there may be a possibility of securing my castles; but I confess it must be done closely and cannily. One of the chief things you are to labour in now, 5 is to get a considerable number of sessioners and advocates to give their opinion that the Covenant is at least against law, if not treasonable.

Charles I to Hamilton, 13 June 1638 in C. Petrie, *The Letters of King Charles I*, 1934, pp. 107–8

5.18

Thus you may see, that I intend not to yield to the demands of those traitors the Covenanters, who I think will declare themselves so by their actions, before I shall do it by my Proclamation; which I shall not be sorry for, so that it be without the personal hurt of you, or any other of my honest servants, or the taking of any English place.   5
This is to show you, that I care not for their affronting or disobeying my Declaration, so that it got not to open mischief, and that I may have some time to end my preparations.

Charles I to Hamilton, 20 June 1638 in C. Petrie, *The Letters of King Charles I*, 1934, p. 109

5.19

To show the world clearly that my taking of arms is to suppress rebellion, and not to impose novelties, but that they are the seekers of them; wherefore if upon the publishing of my Declaration a protestation should follow, I should think it would rather do right than wrong to my cause: and for their calling a Parliament or   5
Assembly without me, I should not much be sorry, for it would the more loudly declare them traitors, and the more justify my actions.

Charles I to Hamilton, 25 June 1638 in C. Petrie, *The Letters of Charles I*, 1934, p. 109

Questions

1   Does The National Covenant [5.14] strike you as the language of treason (see **5.18**) or of rebellion (see **5.19**)?
2   Does document **5.15** strike you as the language of treason and rebellion?
3   How far do documents **5.16–5.19** confirm the view of Charles I which you have formed earlier in the book?
4   Did Charles have any choice but to raise an army against the Convenanters?
5   Turn back to documents **5.1** and **5.2**. Do you feel that these are wildly inappropriate judgements on the period 1629–37? If so, why did these authors write what they did?
6   Kevin Sharpe has written that in the Personal Rule, Charles I 'embarked upon an ambitious renovation of the fabric of Church and

State' and that 'time might well' have 'seasoned and formed minds to comply with public necessities'. Does this chapter bear out those judgements?

7   Theodore Rabb has written that 'resistance to Charles' policy was inevitable and the Scots war was thus the occasion, not the cause, of confrontation and civil war'. Does the material in this chapter help you to decide whether he is right?

In 1639 Charles sent an English army to subdue the Scots. It was defeated. He retained the initiative. He could make a humiliating peace with the Scots and resume the Personal Rule or he could recall the English Parliament and see how far it would support him against the Scots. Only when he dismissed the Short Parliament for being inadequately helpful, but still attempted a second military campaign against the Covenanters, did his control of events falter. The Scots did not wait for him to come to them – they invaded and occupied the North of England. As Charles' army crumbled, the Scots made the summons of an English Parliament to pay their costs, a precondition for returning home. The Long Parliament met with unparalleled freedom to negotiate with the King and to seek redress of grievances.

6 Charles I and the outbreak of civil war 1640–2

When the Long Parliament met in the autumn of 1640, there was a profound sense of tension and of grim opportunity. There is virtually no evidence that anyone – King, ministers, or parliamentary critics – recognized or feared that England was on the brink of civil war. The King had been defeated by the Scots who had occupied the North of England, and they had refused to go home until their war costs were paid by a grant from the English Parliament. This gave Charles' critics a once-for-all opportunity to get things right. They appear to have assumed that the main steps to be taken were:

1 the punishment of the 'evil counsellors' of the 1630s
2 the appointment of responsible ministers (from amongst themselves) to pursue responsible policies
3 measures to ensure that there would be regular parliaments for the future
4 major reforms of the Church, including a massive curtailing of the bishops' powers, if not their outright abolition

Most of these objectives had been obtained by the summer of 1641, and peace was then signed with the Scots (Charles going to Edinburgh to ratify it in September 1641), the troops then returning home and disbanding. Yet far from a return of stability and 'balance', the political temperature climbed throughout the summer of 1641 amidst a welter of mutual recrimination, each side accusing the other of bad faith and of 'arbitrary' behaviour. This is an immensely complex period, and there is not space here to tell the full story of these years. It is vital that you study this chapter *after* gaining a background knowledge of the great and dramatic sequence of events between the summoning of the Long Parliament and the outbreak of war in the late summer/early autumn of 1642. There were four basic phases.

1 In the first phase, down to May 1641, the emphasis was on the investigation and punishment of the King's ministers: half the Privy Council was arrested, dismissed, or chose to flee abroad; the Earl of Strafford was attainted by Parliament and executed; Archbishop Laud was impeached and locked up in the Tower awaiting a full trial. Only one major

piece of legislation was pursued, an Act requiring Charles to summon a new Parliament at least every third year. A formidable body of criticisms of Church government was gathered, and petitions calling for the abolition of episcopacy were given a sympathetic hearing in the Commons. Indeed by May 1641 the Lower House, but not the Upper, was ready to suspend episcopacy and to introduce a temporary system of Church government rule by a Board of clergy and lay (gentry) commissioners in each county.

2 In the second phase, from May to September 1641, Parliament abolished the instruments of 'prerogative' government – Star Chamber, High Commission, etc. But it failed to agree on the best means for providing long-term financial support for the Crown, and failed to make progress in Church reform. There was increasing deadlock between the two Houses, and evidence of a strong backlash in the Commons against radical Puritan schemes.

3 From October 1641 to March 1642 there was a rapid breakdown of trust on all sides. The King was increasingly suspected of attempting to organize a military coup against the Parliament. The Rebellion of Irish Catholics (in the early months of rebellion perhaps 3,000 Protestants were massacred) raised an acute problem: the need to organize an army of reconquest. But who was to control that army? Desperate to keep the people's minds concentrated on the King's record, the Commons pushed through and published a comprehensive inventory of the past misdeeds of his government (*The Grand Remonstrance*), which culminated in a demand that Parliament should have the right to veto all royal appointments. In order to get its measures through either House, and especially through the House of Lords, leading critics of the King increasingly came to rely on mass picketing of Westminster by angry and determined (but disciplined) crowds of apprentices and citizens. After the fiasco of his attempt to arrest five members (actually six: five in the Commons and one in the Lords) in January 1642, and feeling physically intimidated by the London crowd, the King went to the North.

4 From then until the unfurling of his banner in August 1642, the country drifted to war. The King increasingly stressed how political paralysis at the centre was causing a collapse of order and the imminence of anarchy; and how Parliament's attacks on the Church were not promoting peaceful change, but were spawning increasingly violent and shocking religious extremism (an end to all State religion, virulent anti-clericalism, iconoclasm, social revolution). Parliament, meanwhile was forced to improvise, to pass 'ordinances', bills which lacked the royal assent, to secure control of the militia, to raise money and ultimately to raise an

army. Their case was simple: the King's mind had been so corrupted by the evil advisers around him that he was not responsible for his actions. Parliament had a duty to protect not only the people but the Crown in the abstract sense, the office of the King, from this 'popish conspiracy'.

In what follows, we will look at the way both sides made their case. Most of the material in this chapter is taken from propaganda in the precise sense: from tracts which claim to be published versions of private exchanges between the King and the Houses, but which were, in fact, designed entirely to present a case to the public. But we have chosen extracts only from tracts which were issued under the personal supervision of the King or by order of the Houses of Parliament. This does not necessarily mean that either side believed what it published: but it tells us something about *how each wanted to be seen* and it may tell us something about *how the King saw himself and Parliament saw itself.*

Charles' bid to retrieve the support of his subjects began by an acceptance of past mistakes. He never made a full and frank confession, and he never volunteered to reveal any skeletons in the closet; but he did accept some responsibility. Document **6.1** is from a royal Declaration on the eve of civil war, but there are several similar earlier confessions. It comes from a review of events since the summoning of the Long Parliament:

6.1

> We took a full and clear prospect of the inconveniences and mischiefs
> which had grown by the long intermission of Parliaments, and by
> departing too much from the known Rule of the Law, to an Arbitrary
> Power, and upon the whole resolved . . . that the measure of our
> Justice and favour by way of reparation, should far exceed the   5
> proportion of the sufferings our good subjects had undergone by Us
> . . . [as an example, Star Chamber had] in excess of jurisdiction or
> tediousness and charge of proceedings, or measure and severity of
> punishment invaded the Laws of the Land and Liberty of the
> subject, by the exercise of an arbitrary power. We pressed not the   10
> reformation of the Court, though erected or settled by Act of
> Parliament in wise time.

> *His Majesty's Declaration To All His Loving Subjects*, **published 12 August 1642**

The King also complimented himself on having so graciously accepted the reforms that the two Houses of Parliament had demanded:

6.2

We shall in a few words pass over . . . the many good laws passed by
our Grace and favour this Parliament for the security of our people:
of which we shall only say this much, that as we have not refused to
pass any Bill presented to us by our Parliament for redress of those
grievances mentioned in the [Grand] Remonstrance, so we have not   5
had a greater Motive for the passing those laws than our own
resolution (grounded upon our observation, and understanding the
state of our Kingdom) to have freed our subjects for the future, from
those pressures which were grievous to them if those laws had not
been propounded which therefore we shall as inviolably maintain, as   10
we look to have our own Rights preserved.

His Majesty's Declaration to all his Loving Subjects, **published
December 1641**

Charles also claimed that he had dismissed the advisers which the two
Houses had complained against, and had appointed men they had recommended to him:

6.3

Of all the imputations so causelessly and unjustly laid upon us by
[Parliament's] Declaration, we must wonder at that charge so
apparently and evidently untrue that such are continually preferred
and countenanced by Us who are friends or favourers, or related unto
the chief authors and actors of that arbitrary power heretofore   5
practised and complained of: and, on the other side, That such as did
appear against it are daily discountenanced and disgraced. We would
know one person that contributed to the Ills of those times or had
dependence upon those that did, whom we do or lately did
countenance or preferred . . . and whether we have not been forward   10
enough to honour and prefer those of the most contrary opinion, how
little comfort soever we have had of those preferments; in bestowing
of which, hereafter we shall be more guided by men's actions than
opinions.

*His Majesty's Answer to a Book Entitled The Declaration or
Remonstrance of the Lords and Commons*, **19 May 1642**

Questions

1   Would you describe the tone of documents **6.1–6.3** as conciliatory?
2   How complete was Charles' apology for past mistakes as represented by **6.1–6.3**?
3   What would a critic of the King's policies in the 1630s have found unacceptable about the tone and content of documents **6.1–6.3**?
4   What might the King have meant by the phrase 'hereafter we shall be more guided by men's actions than opinions' **[6.3, lines 13–14]**?
5   'Too little and too late.' Do Charles' concessions go far enough?
6   Referring to earlier chapters, what 'inconveniences and mischiefs' **[6.1, line 1]** and 'departing too much from the known Rule of the Law' **[line 3]** would you cite from 1625 to 1640?

As well as defending his own record, Charles accused the Houses of violations of his rights and of the liberties they claimed to have been elected to preserve. Documents **6.4** and **6.5** represent a case study of the bitter exchanges in the months before war broke out. At the end of the war with Scotland in 1640, most of Charles' ammunition and military supplies lay stockpiled in Hull. Control of those supplies would be a vital asset if it came to civil war. As the King moved North in the spring of 1642, Parliament, sensing the danger, sent a local MP, Sir John Hotham, as their governor. When Charles arrived at the gates of Hull, he found them shut against him. By what right could Parliament appoint garrison commanders, or deny him access to an English town? The King went on the verbal offensive:

6.4

> We rather expected . . . that you should have given us an account why a Garrison hath been placed in our town of Hull without our consent and soldiers billeted there against law and the express words of the Petition of Right . . . We would gladly be informed, why our own inclination (on the general rumour of the designs of the papists   5
> in the Northern parts) was not thought sufficient ground for us to put a person of Honour, fortune, and unblemished reputation, into a town and fort of our own, where our own Magazine lay; and yet the same rumour was warrant enough for you to commit the town and fort (without our consent) to the hands of Sir John Hotham, with a   10
> power unagreeable to the law of the land or the liberty of the subject.

> *His Majesty's Answer to the Petition of the Lords and Commons for Leave to remove the Magazine at Hull to the Tower of London*, **printed in April 1642**

This is how the Houses replied:

6.5

Admitting His Majesty had indeed had a property in the Town and
Magazine of Hull, who doubts not but that a Parliament may dispose
of anything wherein His Majesty or any subjects hath a right, in such
a way, as that the kingdom may not be exposed to hazard or danger
thereby, which is our case in the disposing of the Town and   5
Magazine of Hull . . . We shall never allow a few private persons
about His Majesty, nor His Majesty himself in his own person and
out of his courts to be Judge of the Law, and that contrary to the
judgment of the Highest Court of judicature . . . [especially] as His
Majesty taketh the measure of what will be for the peace and   10
happiness of the kingdom from some few ill-affected persons about
him, contrary to the advice and judgment of the Great Council of
Parliament.

A Remonstrance or Declaration of the Lords and Commons . . ., **26 May**
1642

Questions

1 How strong do you find the King's case in **6.4**?
2 How strong do you find the Parliament's case in **6.5**?
3 Comment on the following two statements about Charles' adventure
 at Hull:
 (i) 'The King's attempt to enter Hull was an unnecessary and
   provocative escalation of tension.'
 (ii) 'Hotham's refusal to let Charles into Hull proved what the King
   was now saying: that it was now the Houses and not he who had
   no respect for Law.'

The King also charged the Houses with failing to condemn, indeed with
condoning mob rule, especially in London. In document **6.6** he character-
izes and then criticizes their refusal to condemn the picketing of Parliament
by large crowds of apprentices and others, protesting against the bishops in
December 1642:

6.6

[They say that] the resort of the citizens to Westminster was as
lawful as the resort of great numbers every day in the term to the
ordinary courts of justice. They know no tumults. Strange! Was the
disorderly appearance of so many thousand people with staves and
swords crying through the streets, Westminster Hall, the passage   5
between both Houses (in so much as the members could hardly pass
to and fro) crying 'No Bishops, Down with the Bishops' no tumult?
What member is there in either House that saw not those numbers
and heard not those cries? And yet lawful assemblies? Were not
several members of either House assaulted, threatened, and ill   10
treated? And yet no tumults? Why made the House of Peers a
declaration, and Sent it down to the house of Commons, if there were
no Tumults? When the attempts were so visible and the threats so
loud to pull down the Abbey at Westminster, had not we cause to
apprehend, That such people might continue their work to   15
Whitehall? Yet no Tumults? . . . We will have justice for those
tumults.

*His Majesty's Answer to a Book Entitled The Declaration or
Remonstrance of the Lords and Commons . . ., 19 May 1642*

Questions

1   Why might Parliament have been reluctant to condemn the 'Tumults'
    of December 1642?
2   Were the Tumults, such as are described in **6.6**, necessarily
    something that would make people more sympathetic to the King?
3   Are the words in **6.6, lines 13–16** anything more than a scare tactic?
    Might the King's apprehension have been realistic?
4   On the evidence presented in **6.5** and **6.6**, had Parliament taken the
    initiative from Charles?

Arguably the King's strongest suit in his bid to regain support was religion.
He distanced himself from Archbishop Laud, whom he allowed to be
imprisoned and whom he did nothing to help (later, in 1644, he made
virtually no effort to save the old man's life when he was tried, convicted
and beheaded by the two Houses). In 1641, he promoted several bishops
and appointed several new ones – almost all opponents of the Archbishop.
He made a number of statements implicitly – even explicitly – critical of the
Church policies of the 1630s; but he stoutly defended the Elizabethan

Church Settlement itself, with diocesan bishops and the Book of Common Prayer. Below [6.7] is one of his most telling statements of his religious policies in these years. It addresses the calls for a completely fresh ecclesiastical settlement:

6.7

Unto that clause which concerneth corruptions (as you style them) in religion, in church government and in discipline, in such unnecessary ceremonies as weak consciences might check: that for any illegal innovations which may have crept in, we shall willingly concur in the removal of them. That if our Parliament shall advise us to call a   5
national synod, which may duly examine such ceremonies as give just cause of offence to any, we shall take it into consideration and apply ourself to give due satisfaction therein; but we are very sorry to hear in such general terms corruption in religion objected, since we are persuaded in our conscience that no church can be found upon earth   10
that professeth the true religion with more purity of doctrine than the Church of England doth, nor where the government and discipline are jointly more beautified and free from superstition, than as they are here established by law, which by the Grace of God we will with constancy maintain in their purity and glory, not only against all   15
invasions of popery, but also from the irreverence of those many schismatics and seperatists wherewith of late this kingdom and this city abounds . . . for the suppression of whom we require your timely aid and active assistance.

His Majesty's Answer to the Petition Accompanying the Declaration (**ie.** the Grand Remonstrance), December 1641

Six months later the message was the same, but the language more violent:

6.8

Is the true Reformed Protestant Church, sealed by the Blood of so many Reverend Martyrs, and established by the wisdom and piety of former blessed Parliaments, dear to them? . . . Let all our good subjects consider and weigh what pregnant arguments they have to fear Innovations in religion, if these desperate persons prevail; when   5
the principal men, to whose care and industry they have committed

the managing of that part, refuse communion with the Church of England as much as the papists do',[1] and have . . . reproached the book of common prayer and government of the Church in their speeches.

[1] a marginal note in the printed tract at this point mentions Lord Saye and Sele by name

His Majesty's Declaration to all his Loving Subjects, **12 August 1642**

Questions

1   Explain and comment on the following phrases:
     (i) 'those many schismatics and separatists' [**6.7, lines 16–17**]
     (ii) 'sealed by the Blood of so many Reverend Martyrs' [**6.8, lines 1–2**]
2   What light do documents **6.7** and **6.8** throw on the King's public position in 1641–2 in respect to (i) Laudianism (ii) Puritanism?
3   In the light of your work in earlier chapters, do you find the tone or content of **6.7** and **6.8** surprising or unsurprising?
4   Why might Charles have added the final phrase of **6.7**?

Charles followed up these accounts of himself as a chastened, wiser and moderate man, by claiming that Parliament had been taken over by an organized group of fanatics:

6.9

[Those responsible for all our troubles are] a faction of Malignant, Schismatical and Ambitious persons, whose design is, and always has been, to alter the frame of the Government both of Church and State, and to subject both King and People to their own lawless arbitrary power and Government.

His Majesty's Answer to a Printed Book, **26 May 1642**

6.10

There is not a particular of which we complain that found not an eminent opposition in both Houses, and yet for the most part not above a moity [= half] of either House present . . . Our quarrel is not against the Parliament but against particular men, whom we

name, and are ready to prove them guilty of High Treason . . .   5
[4 Peers and 14 Members of the House of Commons are then
named].

His Majesty's Declaration, 12 August 1642

On 22 August 1642, Charles raised his standard at Nottingham. It was a
declaration of war on Parliament. But three days later he issued the
following Declaration, either seeking a last-minute settlement or at least
wanting to be thought to be seeking one.

6.11

We have, with unspeakable grief of heart, long beheld the distractions
of this our kingdom. Our very soul is full of anguish, until we may
find some remedy to prevent the miseries which are ready to
overwhelm this whole nation with a civil war . . . We have thought fit
to propound to you that some fit persons may be by you enabled to   5
treat with the like number to be authorized by us, in such manner,
and with such freedom of debate as may best tend to that happy
conclusion which all men desire, the peace of the kingdom . . .
Nothing shall be wanting on our part which may advance the true
Protestant religion, oppose Popery and superstition, secure the law of   10
the land (upon which is built as well our just prerogative and liberty
of the subject), confirm all just power and privileges of Parliament
and render us and our people happy.

Charles I, *Declaration from Nottingham*, 25 August 1642

Questions

1   Using your wider knowledge of the period, do you think there is any
    justice in the charges levelled in **6.9** and **6.10**?
2   Why might Charles I have issued **6.11** only three days after declaring
    war on Parliament?
3   Looking back over documents **6.1–6.11** would you agree that 'Charles
    I was successful in occupying the middle ground of English politics'?
4   Do *you* think that Charles believed his own propaganda?

Very shortly afterwards, Charles wrote to the Earl of Newcastle, his Northern commander, concerning who should serve in his army [6.12b]. This appeared to contradict a solemn assurance he had given only weeks before [6.12a].

6.12a

Whereas . . . We have found it necessary to raise and levy forces . . . Lest any popish recusants should presume to offer to serve us herein, or procure themselves to be listed, as officers or soldiers in our army, without our knowledge, and to the end that our intention herein may be clearly known, That whereas one principal aim of raising these   5
forces, is, for the defence and maintainance of the true Protestant Religion, We may not be served by Papists.

Charles I, 12 August 1642, in *Stuart Royal Proclamations*, **vol. II, pp. 795–6**

6.12b

This is to tell you that this rebellion is grown to that height that I must not look what opinion men are who at the time are willing and able to serve me. Therefore I do not only permit but command you to make use of all my loving subjects' services, without examining their consciences (more than their loyalty to me) as you shall find   5
most to conduce to the upholding of my just regal power.

Charles I to the Earl of Newcastle, 23 September 1642, in C. Petrie, *Letters of King Charles I*, **1934, p. 128**

Questions

1   Who might Charles have had in mind as the 'loving subjects' whose consciences must not be examined in **6.12b, line 4**?
2   How do you account for the contradiction between **6.12a** and **6.12b**?
3   Is the material in **6.12a** and **6.12b** relevant or irrelevant to your answer to question 2 on page 101?
4   Parliamentary propagandists and some of Charles' supporters thought that **6.12b** undermined the credibility of such declarations as **6.11**. Do you agree?

We now turn to look at Parliament's case against the King. It was very simple and it was endlessly reiterated: the King was not a reformed character. He was still surrounded by 'evil councillors', he intended to jettison, at the earliest opportunity, all the concessions he had gracelessly conceded in 1641, and fresh checks had to be imposed on his freedom to choose his own advisers. Only when he was faithfully counselled, and only when the Church was reconstituted along more thoroughly Protestant lines, would the nation be safe. The classic account of a King, not himself evil, but misled and confused, comes in the preamble to *The Grand Remonstrance* [6.13]. It is a catalogue of misgovernment since Charles came to the throne (98 clauses), a list of the remedies already attempted by Parliament (65 clauses), and a further list of tasks still to be accomplished (41 clauses).

6.13

The Commons in this present Parliament assembled, having . . . for the space of twelve months wrestled with great dangers and fears . . . which had overwhelmed and extinguished the liberty, peace and prosperity of this kingdom . . . do yet find an abounding malignity and opposition in those parties and factions who have been the cause   5
of those evils, and do still labour to cast aspersions upon that which hath been done . . . The root of all this mischief we find to be a malignant and pernicious design of subverting the fundamental laws and principles of government, upon which the religion and justice of this kingdom are firmly established. The actors and promoters hereof   10
have been: 1. The jesuited Papists who hate the laws, as the obstacles of that change and subversion of religion which they so much long for. 2. The Bishops and the corrupt part of the clergy, who cherish formality and superstition as the natural effects and more probable supports of their own ecclesiastical tyranny and usurpation. 3. Such   15
counsellors and courtiers as for private ends have engaged themselves to further the interests of some foreign princes or states. The common principles by which they moulded and governed all their particular counsels and actions were these. First, to maintain continual differences and discontents between the King and the   20
people upon questions of prerogative and liberty that so they might have the advantage of siding with him . . . Second to suppress the purity and power of religion, the greatest impediment to that change which they sought to introduce . . . A third . . to cherish the Arminian part in those points wherein they agree with the Papists, to   25

multiply and enlarge the difference between the common Protestants and those whom they call Puritans . . . A fourth, to disaffect the King to Parliaments by slander and false imputations . . .

The Grand Remonstrance, **presented to the King, 1 December 1641**

As the crisis deepened, Parliament had to articulate its terms for a settlement short of war. It did so in *The Nineteen Propositions*. Two crucial items were as follows:

6.14

1 That the Lords and others of your Majesty's Privy Council and such great officers and Ministers of State, either at home or beyond the seas, may be put from your Privy Council, and from those offices and employments, excepting such as shall be approved by both Houses of Parliament.

5

8 That your Majesty will be pleased to consent that such a reformation be made of the Church government and liturgy, as both Houses of Parliament shall advise.

The Nineteen Propositions, **1 June 1642**

Questions

1   Have you, in your wider reading, found any evidence to support any of the charges in *The Grand Remonstrance* [6.13]?
2   Consider whether the framers of **6.13** can really have believed what they were writing.
3   Charles called the first of the Nineteen Propositions 'an attempt to unking me and set up a popular sovereignty'. Do you think he was right?
4   Because of the shortage of space, we could only give short extracts from the Nineteen Propositions [6.14]. If you have access to them in a fuller form (see Bibliography, page 118; Collections of documents by S. R. Gardiner and J. P. Kenyon), look at the whole document. Do you think we were right to call these the most important articles?

One problem for Charles in attempting to present himself as a moderate and reformed character was that he was constantly accused, with varying degrees of truth, of plotting military coups to re-establish his personal authority. In May 1641, Parliament uncovered a plot by a group of army officers (who had served in the campaigns against Scotland) to seize the Tower, effect the escape of Strafford and to threaten Parliament with dissolution (there was a subsidiary and wilder plot to seize a south-coast port as a prelude to bringing over a French army). The parliamentary commission accused the Queen of complicity (with good reason); but they could not pin down the King. (We now know that he was thoroughly implicated, but the plotters protected him). In October he was involved in a plot to arrest leading Covenanters as they sat in the Scottish Parliament, but again he could not be *proved* to have instigated it. In November, he was accused of instigating the Irish Rebellion (we can be ninety-nine per cent sure he was innocent of this charge). But in January 1642 his personal appearance in the Chamber of the House of Commons with an armed escort, seeking to arrest five leading MPs on charges of treason, left no doubt as to his vengeful nature (although those MPs who supported him in the war were to argue that he had been sorely provoked, even if it was illegal and unwise). The five MPs, forewarned, had fled.

The following documents [**6.15** and **6.16**] relate to two of these incidents – the Irish rebellion and the Attempt on the Five Members. Document **6.15** is a Declaration made by Phelim O'Neale who led the Irish rebels:

6.15

To all the Catholics of the Roman party, both English and Irish,
within the Kingdom of Ireland . . . be it hereby known unto you that
the King . . . has signified unto us by his Commission . . . divers
great and heinous affronts that the English Protestants, especially the
Parliament, have published against the royal person and prerogative   5
and also against our Catholic friends . . . [His Commission commands
us] to advise and consult together . . . for the ordering, settling and
effecting of this great work, mentioned and directed to you in our
Letters, and to use all politick ways and means possibly to possess
yourselves, for our use and safety, of all the Forts, Castles and places   10
of strength and defence within the said kingdom, and also to arrest
and seize the goods, estates and persons of all the English Protestants
within the same kingdom . . .

**From the Declaration of Phelim O'Neale, 4 November 1641, printed
in J. Rushworth, *Historical Collections*, part III, vol. I, pp. 400–1 (the
printer in error used page numbers 385–416 twice: this passage is
from the second lot of pages 400–1!)**

Document **6.16** consists of just two items from a long account by Parliament of the way evil counsellors had plotted against the Long Parliament, seeking papal finance, fomenting war with the Scots etc.

6.16

(i) That the Rebellion in Ireland was framed and contrived here in England, and that the English Papists should have risen about the same time, we have several testimonies and advertisements from Ireland . . . The boldness of the Irish rebels in affirming they do nothing but by authority from the King; that they call themselves the   5
Queen's army; that the prey or booty which they take from the English, they marke with the Queen's mark.

(ii) The false and scandalous accusations . . . tendered to the Parliament by your Majesty's own command, endeavoured to be justified in the City, by your own presence and persuasion, and to be   10
put in execution upon their persons, by your Majesty's demand of the [Five Members] in the House of Commons, in so terrible and violent manner, as far exceeded all former breaches of Privileges of Parliament, acted by your Majesty or any of your predecessors. And whatever your own intentions were, divers bloody and desperate   15
persons which attended your Majesty, discovered their affections and resolutions to have massacred and destroyed the Members of the House . . .

Declaration of the Lords and Commons, **2 March 1642**

Questions

1   Why might Irish rebels **[6.15]** have claimed a royal commission for their rising (something no Irish Catholic rebels before or since have ever done)?

2   In document **6.16**, how far does Parliament blame, or exonerate, the King for complicity with the Irish rebels?

3   Some MPs clearly believed that Charles was involved in the Irish rebellion. Why might they have believed this?

4   Evaluate **6.16** as a piece of propaganda, looking at both its tone and content.

5   Put yourself in the position of Charles I's advisers at the end of 1641. Would you have tried to dissuade him from going to Parliament to

arrest the Five Members? Once the Attempt had failed, what public statement would you have advised him to put out?

6 From your wider knowledge, consider what would have happened if the Five Members had been present and Charles had arrested them.

As document **6.16** suggests, Parliament was especially sensitive about the role and influence of the Queen. The following documents [**6.17** and **6.18**] may suggest to you that such fears were well-founded. Charles had grown to love and trust Henrietta-Maria more and more after some stormy early years to their marriage. She was a devout Catholic and was principally concerned to help her English co-religionists. It may also have been relevant that she was the daughter of Henri IV of France who had had to fight his way to the throne at the end of forty years of civil war in France, and who had reintroduced strong authoritarian rule which had worked. Documents **6.17a–d** consist of extracts from reports by the (Catholic) ambassadors of Venice to their masters; documents **6.18a–c** consist of short extracts from letters that Henrietta-Maria wrote to her husband from Holland in 1642. She had gone there to pawn the Crown jewels to help to finance his military activities as civil war approached.

6.17a

[Parliament's actions are] very distasteful to His Majesty and especially to the Queen who is full of generous spirit and shows that she feels very strongly at seeing her husband not only deprived of his most faithful ministers but so effectively despised by his own subjects. For this reason, she never ceases to urge him to throw himself into desperate courses and it is to be feared he may at last lose patience and listen to her, with danger of more serious consequences.   5

Giovanni Giustinian, writing from London to Venice, 11 January 1641

6.17b

The Queen of England, with her own hand, has written to Cardinal Barberino lamenting the unhappy state of the kingdom and her husband, and begging for a loan of 500,000 Crowns, under the plea that the catholic Faith, protected from that quarter, will derive great benefit.

Anzolo Contarini, writing from Rome to Venice, 2 February 1641

6.17c

The Queen also, unable to bear any longer seeing the contempt of the
people for her husband and herself . . . has decided to cross to
Holland, ostensibly to take over her daughter, the bride of the young
Prince there . . . The Parliamentarians, are of opinion that with the
Queen away it will not be difficult for them to direct the King's will   5
with complete freedom . . . The Queen announces that she will stay a
year in Holland, and will return to England when the ornaments of
his original authority are restored to the king, otherwise she talks of
going to France. I am advised most confidentially by a person of
great credit and influence that the Queen's journey is taken in secret   10
concert with France and covers very extensive designs.

Giustinian, writing from London to Venice, 20 February 1642

6.17d

The Queen told me positively that to settle affairs it was necessary to
unsettle them first, as she considered it impossible to reestablish her
husband's authority in any other way.

**Giustinian, writing from London to Venice, 21 February 1642. All
four extracts (translated from Italian) are in the *Calendar of State
Papers Venetian 1640–2*, pp. 112, 117, 294, 295**

6.18a

Assuredly, God will assist us, and whatever may be said to you, do
not break your resolution, but follow it constantly and do not lose
time . . . When you come to York, if you find the country well
affected, Hull must absolutely be had. If you cannot you must go to
Newcastle, and if you find that that is not safe, go to Berwick, for it   5
is necessary to have a seaport, for reasons that I will send to inform
you of . . .

Henrietta-Maria to Charles, from the Hague, 15 March 1642

6.18b

A report is current here, that you are returning to London or near it.
I believe nothing of it, and hope that you are more constant in your
resolutions; you have already learned to your cost, that want of

perseverance in your designs has ruined you. But if it be so, adieu: I
must pray to God, for assuredly you will never change my resolution   5
to retire into a convent, for I can never trust myself to those persons
who would be your directors nor to you, since you would have
broken your promise to me . . . The money is not ready, for on your
jewels, they will lend nothing. I am forced to pledge all my little
ones, for the great ones nothing can be had here.

Henrietta-Maria to Charles, undated, but March 1642

6.18c

It is also to be feared that the Parliament will take a path more
moderate in appearance, but in effect worse for you. Wherefore, that
ought to be well considered. A report is current here, that you will
grant the militia for one year, but your letter relieves me of that fear,
for you assure me to the contrary.

**Henrietta-Maria to Charles, undated, but probably April 1642. All
extracts are in M. A. E. Green (ed.), *Letters of Queen Henrietta Maria*,
1859, pp. 52–3, 55–7, 61**

Questions

1   Explain the following terms:
    (i) 'the ornaments of his original authority' [**6.17c, lines 7–8**].
    (ii) 'it was necessary to unsettle them first' [**6.17d, lines 1–2**].
    (iii) 'that want of perseverence in your designs has ruined you'
        [**6.18b, lines 3–4**].
2   What do documents **6.17** and **6.18** tell you about Henrietta-Maria?
3   What do these documents tell you about Charles I?
4   What insights do these documents provide into the relationship of
    Charles I and Henrietta-Maria?

We ended the section on the King's view of the crisis with a Declaration he
issued in August 1642 [**6.11**]. We end this chapter with Parliament's
passionate attack on Charles' government, issued earlier in the same
month:

6.19

By the concurrence and assistance of papists, an ambitious and
discontented clergy, delinquents obnoxious to the justice of

Parliament; and some ill-affected persons of the Nobility and Gentry; who out of their desire of a dissolute liberty, apprehend and would keep off the reformation intended by the Parliament. These persons   5
have conspired together to ruin this Parliament, which alone hath set a stop to that violence so long intended; and often attempted for the alteration of religion, and subversion of the laws and liberties of the kingdom. How far are we plunged in a miserable expectation of most evil days, and how fast this growing mischief prevailed upon us   10
before the Parliament, needs not now be declared it being so fresh and bleeding in every man's memory; religion was made but form and outside; and those who made conscience to maintain the substance and purity of it, whether clergy or others, were discountenced and oppressed, as the great enemies of the state. The   15
Laws were no defence, nor protection of any man's right, all was subject to will and power, which imposed what payments they thought fit, to drain the subjects' purse, and supply those necessities, which evil counsellors had brought upon the king, or gratify such as were instruments in promoting those illegal and oppressive courses.   20
They who yielded and complied were countenanced and advanced, all others disgraced and kept under: that so men's minds made poor and base, and their liberties lost and gone, they might be ready to let go their religion, whensoever it should be resolved to alter it, which was and still is the great design, and all else made use of, but as   25
instrumentary and subservient to it.

A Declaration of the Lords and Commons, 8 August 1642

Questions

1   How persuasive is **6.19** as a piece of propaganda?
2   'Both King and Parliament went to war in defence of a conspiracy theory. Both theories were patently absurd.' Do you agree?
3   'Parliament went to war to protect the constitution of England and to change the religion of Englishmen.' Does this chapter bear out that judgement?
4   To what extent were Parliament's grievances against the misgovernment of one man: Charles I?
5   The events of 1640–2 need to be set against government in Church and State from 1625 to 1640. Do they demonstrate the inevitability of historical forces?

7 Judgement

Pressure of space has led us to bring this book to an end in 1642. It would take as much space again to provide the contexts within which to make sense of the events that led to Charles I's trial and execution in January 1649. In this chapter, we will just round off the story and then offer five contrasting assessments of Charles' aims and failings written by modern scholars.

Charles had a good war. He displayed qualities of leadership and courage, and although he was too tolerant of disputes amongst his regional commanders (which led to costly lack of co-operation), he cannot be blamed for his defeat. Parliament had a stronger strategic and logistic position; it had financial resources that held out better in a long war; it had decisive help from 20,000 Scots in the winter of 1643–4 and the summer of 1644; and it had control of the navy.

By 1646 the King's military position had collapsed and he surrendered himself first to the Scots and then to the English Parliament. Throughout 1646 and 1647 he showed a reluctant willingness to negotiate; but those who treated with him were left with an enduring sense that he was negotiating in bad faith. He may have been deliberately stalling in the hope that the divisions amongst his enemies would work increasingly to his advantage. Alternatively, Parliament's non-negotiable religious terms (the abolition of bishops and the Book of Common Prayer) may have been one of those good causes he believed he could never yield. However, in January 1648, he signed a treaty with the Scots (themselves disillusioned with their English allies) and launched a second war. This had the result of polarizing his enemies further, and a minority, backed by the army leaders, decided that enough was enough. Claiming that Charles was 'a man of blood', one who had opposed God's cause and plunged the nation into blood and suffering, the army demanded that he be destroyed in order to atone for his sins. The outcome was one favoured by only a tiny minority of the nation – and regicide and the abolition of monarchy did not introduce an age of liberty. After an eleven-year Interregnum, the Stuarts were restored.

On the eve of his execution, Charles wrote a private letter to his eldest son, the future Charles II [7.1]. You may well believe that here, if any-where, Charles would pour out his true feelings; you must remember that what he writes here might have been shaped by the traumas of civil war.

7.1

I had rather you should be Charles *le bon*, than *le grand*, good than
great; I hope God hath designed you to be both; having so early put
you into that exercise of His grace and gifts bestowed upon you . . .

Above all, I would have you already, well grounded and settled in
your religion, the best profession of which I have ever esteemed that   5
of the Church of England, in which you have been educated . . .
Your fixation in matters of religion will not be more necessary for
your soul's than your kingdom's peace, when God shall bring you to
them.

For I have observed, that the devil of rebellion doth commonly   10
turn himself into an angel of reformation; and the old serpent can
pretend new lights, when some men's consciences accuse them for
sedition and faction, they stop its mouth with the name and noise of
religion; when piety pleads for peace and patience, they cry out zeal . . .

The next main hinge on which your prosperity will depend and   15
move, is that of civil justice, wherein the settled laws of these
kingdoms, to which you are rightly heir, are the most excellent rules
you can govern by, which by an admirable temperament give very
much to subjects industry, liberty, and happiness . . . Your
prerogative is best showed and exercised in remitting rather than in   20
exacting the rigour of the laws; there being nothing worse than legal
tyranny . . .

I do require and entreat you as your father and your king that you
never suffer your heart to receive the least check against or
disaffection from the true religion established in the Church of   25
England. I tell you I have tried it, and have concluded it to be the
best in the world, . . . keeping the middle way between the pomp of
superstitious tyranny and the meanness of fantastic anarchy.

Nor would I have you entertain any aversion or dislike of
Parliaments, which, in their right constitution with freedom and   30
honour, will never hinder or diminish your greatness, but will rather
be an interchanging of love, loyalty, and confidence, between a prince
and his people. Nor would the events of this black Parliament have
been other than such (however much biased by factions in the
elections) if it had been preserved from the insolencies of popular   35
dictates, and tumultuary impressions . . .

**Letter of Charles I, 29 January 1649, in C. Petrie, *Letters of King
Charles I*, 1934, pp. 263–271**

Questions

1   Do you consider this letter [7.1] an important guide to Charles' lifetime beliefs?
2   Are you surprised that Charles put so much emphasis on upholding the Church of England?
3   What do you make of Charles' view that there is 'nothing worse than legal tyranny' [lines 21–2]?
4   Is the account of Parliament in the final paragraph at odds with Charles' view expressed elsewhere in this book or his view as you have encountered it in your wider reading?

We conclude with five extracts from recent works on Charles I. Extract 7.2, by Charles Carlton, uses psycho-analytical models to understand the mainsprings of Charles' personality; 7.3, by John Kenyon, offers a more conventional historical assessment of his personality. Extracts 7.4 and 7.5, by Lawrence Stone and Kevin Sharpe, are sharply contrasting accounts of Charles' policies. According to Stone he was leading a reaction to change; according to Sharpe he was offering dynamic and innovative responses to the problems he inherited. Finally, 7.6 is a startling challenge to traditional interpretations by Conrad Russell, who argues that it was Charles I who made war on his people, not his people-in-parliament on Charles I.

7.2

In psychological terms Charles' early years had produced an overdeveloped superego that bottled up his inner tensions. Charles tried to protect himself by seeking affection, currying favour, becoming withdrawn, displaying deference rare in an heir, and above all, by submitting. Thus when he became king he expected similar   5
behaviour, demanded a similar sacrifice, and insisted upon as great and painful a loyalty as he had been forced to yield. An authoritarian personality, Charles was incapable of conceding at a time when compromises were desperately demanded from the English monarchy. He was full of outward self-certainty (manifest in such doctrines as   10
divine right) that only intense inner doubt can engender . . .

C. Carlton, in J. G. A. Pocock (ed.), *Three British Revolutions 1641, 1688, 1776*, 1981, pp. 185–6

7.3

Charles I is also a man of considerable contradictions and
controversy. The Whig historians, notably Gardiner, portray him as
sick in mind and essentially stupid, beneath a veneer of
intellectualism and culture. But the prince who took the lead in the
Parliaments of 1621 and 1624 was quick-witted enough, and the man   5
who composed the *Eikon Basilike* was very far from being stupid . . .
Charles had an aggressive, unsubtle self-confidence which had been
encouraged, if anything, by his dealings with [those] Parliaments. His
were the politics of confrontation, not discussion . . . He was not as
vocal as his father about the Divine Right of Kings, but he believed   10
in it more firmly, and was not prepared to compromise as James had
been. James' beliefs, in fact were largely a reaction to Scots
conditions, and [in England] he was willing to qualify them. Charles
took them over unaltered as a blueprint for the English constitution.

J. P. Kenyon, *Stuart England*, revised edn, 1985, pp. 100–1

7.4

During the decade before the crash in 1640, a series of developments
took place which may be regarded as precipitants of crisis, for they
brought the collapse of governmental institutions from the realm of
possibility to that of probability . . .

    In the first place the Crown associated itself wholeheartedly with a   5
vigorous religious reaction guided and driven furiously forward by
Archbishop Laud. The latter saw Church and State as two
beleaguered garrisons which needed to unite against their enemies,
and by cementing the alliance he ensured that the fall of the one
would inevitably drag the other down with it . . .   10

    Parallel to this reaction in religion was a reaction in politics in the
degree of participation allowed to the traditional freeholder electorate
and the traditional gentry representatives . . . [in 1629] he dissolved
Parliament and proclaimed his intention of ruling without it. He then
proceeded to raise taxes without consent by juggling with the letter of   15
the law and by perverting residual prerogative powers of the Crown
for emergency action in moments of national danger. Medieval
precedents were dredged up to allow the Crown to fine large
numbers of the gentry for their failure to take up knighthood, and to

fine selected numbers of noblemen for ancient encroachments on the 20
royal forests – a move which involved a serious challenge to the right
to property . . .

In addition . . . Charles set out to enforce a social reaction, to put
the lid on the social mobility he found so distasteful . . . He drove
the gentry and nobility out of London back to their rural retreats 25
where he thought they belonged . . . and did all he could to bolster
up noble privileges and to reinforce the hierarchy of ranks . . .

Lastly Charles got himself involved in economic reaction. Guild
organization was imposed from above on numerous crafts and trades,
the purpose of which was to establish strict royal control over the 30
industrial and artisan class of small masters . . .

In short, the objective of 'Thorough' was a deferential, strictly
hierarchical, socially stable, paternalist absolutism based on a close
union of Church and Crown.

L. Stone, *Causes of the English Revolution*, 1972, pp. 118–27

7.5

The style of Charles' court reflected the image of the king: formal
and reserved. But it was not only in the sphere of morality and
manners that the concern for order was revealed. Charles instigated a
programme of reform and retrenchment at Court, a programme
which, if never very successful, at least curtailed the curve of rising 5
extravagance . . . The concern with order was not confined to the
Court. Indeed it is important to understand that for Charles I the
Court was not to be . . . a retreat from the world of reality, but
rather a model for the reformed government of Church and State.
Fear of the collapse of all authority and the dislocation of society 10
directed the king's attention to the reordering of society and
government. Where there were no laws, the Council was to act to
tackle problems, where statutes had already prescribed measures, the
Council was to ensure that they were enforced. The Book of Orders
. . . is remarkable as an innovative attempt to deal with . . . the 15
symptoms of dearth and poverty . . .

The reestablishment of authority in the localities, in the hands of
the most important local families, was a central beam of his social
reconstruction . . .

It is in the context of these concerns, of this looking back to an 20

(idealised) society of harmony and deference that we should understand Charles' religious policy. If order was Charles I's private religion, then it behoved all the more that the religion of the realm be ordered. Gardiner, in a perceptive phrase, captured the central tenet of royal policy: 'the incongruity of dirt and disorder with sacred   25
things' . . .

When he decided to govern without parliaments, Charles I did not resign himself to a hand-to-mouth struggle for mere survival; he embarked upon an ambitious renovation of the fabric of Church and state.

Kevin Sharpe, in H. Tomlinson (ed.), *Before the English Civil War 1603–42*, **1983, pp. 59–61**

7.6

Civil Wars are like other quarrels: it takes two to make them. It is, then, something of a curiosity that we possess no full analysis of why Charles I chose to fight a Civil War in 1642 . . . If we look carefully at the slow process of escalation by which the political crisis of 1640 was transformed into the Civil War of 1642, it was usually Charles   5
who raised the stakes by introducing threats of force. It was Charles, in August 1642, who raised his standard and legally began a state of war. This fact repeated a pattern which was already visible. In January 1642, it was Charles who left London, and thereby first separated the combatants into two armed camps. The physical   10
division of the political community caused by the rival summonses to rally to York and to Westminster made an enormous contribution to the creation of an atmosphere in which Civil War became a real possibility. Moreover, the week before Charles left London, it was he who brought armed guards to arrest the Five Members, not the Five   15
Members who brought armed guards to Whitehall Palace . . .

Charles's opponents . . . were not aiming at Civil War, though from Charles's point of view their actions were at least as provocative as if they had been. His opponents were following a strategy with precedents going back at least to Simon de Montfort, in which the   20
object was to impersonalise royal authority by putting it into the hands of a Council and great officers to be nominated in Parliament and answerable to Parliament . . .

Conrad Russell, 'Why did Charles I fight the Civil War?', *History Today*, **June 1984, pp. 31–2**

Questions

1 Are extracts **7.2–7.6** largely presenting a common view of Charles, or incompatible ones?
2 What evidence *for* and *against* each of the above views have you encountered in this book (and elsewhere)?
3 'Charles I caused the civil war: he was not the only cause, but his mistakes were the ones that determined when and how that civil war broke out.' Using evidence from this book, discuss this judgement.

Bibliography

Bibliographies

G. Davies and M. Keeler, *Bibliography of British History: Stuart Period, 1603–1714*, 1970. Comprehensive for books and articles published before 1962. J. Morrill, *Seventeenth-Century Britain*, 1980, contains 867 books and 478 articles mostly published between 1962 and 1980. For more recent publications, see the *Royal Historical Society Annual Bibliography of British and Irish History* [annual since 1975, edited by G. Elton (1975–85), and D. Palliser, (1986–)].

Biographies

C. Carlton, *Charles I*, 1981
P. Gregg, *King Charles I*, 1981

Surveys

The following surveys can all be recommended for general background reading and contain information and ideas relevant to most or all chapters in this book. They are in ascending order of conceptual sophistication. The first three are the most accessible.
R. Lockyer, *Tudor and Stuart England* (only revised edn 1985 recommended)
B. Coward, *The Stuart Age*, 1978
J. Kenyon, *The Stuarts* (only 2nd edn, 1986 recommended)
C. Russell, *The Crisis of Parliaments 1509–1660*, 1971
R. Ashton, *The English Civil War 1603–49*, 1978
D. Hirst, *Authority and Conflict 1603–58*, 1986
J. Sommerville, *Politics and Ideology 1603–40*, 1986

Collections of documents

S. R. Gardiner, *Constitutional Documents of the Puritan Revolution, 1625–60* (3rd edn 1906; many reprints)
J. P. Kenyon, *The Stuart Constitution*, 2nd edn 1986
A. Hughes, *Seventeenth-Century England: a changing Culture*, 1980

Period 1625–29

C. Russell, *Parliaments and English Politics 1621–29*, 1979
S. White, *Sir Edward Coke and the 'Grievances of the Commonwealth'*, 1979

D. Hirst, 'The Privy Council and the Problem of Enforcement', *Journal of British Studies*, 1978
R. Crust, 'Charles I and the Forced Loan', *Journal of British Studies*, 1982
C. Russell, 'The Early Career of John Pym' in *The English Commonwealth 1547–1640*, ed. Peter Clark *et al*, 1979
P. Salt, 'The Parliamentary Career of Sir Thomas Wentworth' *Northern, History*, vol. XVI, 1980

Period 1629–40

E. Cope, *Politics Without Parliament*, 1987
H. Tomlinson (ed.), *Before the English Civil War 1603–42*, 1983, Chapters 3, 5 and 7
C. Russell (ed.), *The Origins of the English Civil War*, 1973, Chapters 1, 3, 4, 6 and 7

The following are of particular value for Chapter 3:
P. Thomas, 'Charles I of England, the Tragedy of Absolutism' in A. G. Dickens (ed.), *The Courts of Europe: Politics, Patronage and Royalty 1400–1800*, 1977
G. Parry, *The Golden Age Restored: the Culture of the Stuart Court*, 1981, especially Chapter 9
M. Butler, *Theatre and Crisis, 1632–42*, 1983

Three books by R. Strong are particularly worth reading on the artistic interests of Charles I:
R. Strong, *Van Dyck: Charles I on Horseback*, 1972
R. Strong, *Britannia Triumphans: Inigo Jones, Rubens and Whitehall Palace*, 1980
R. Strong, *Henry, Prince of Wales and England's Lost Renaissance*, 1986

The best introductions to Laudianism are:
C. Russell (ed.), *The Origins of the English Civil War*, 1973, Chapter 4
J. S. McGee, 'William Laud and the Outward Face of Religion' in *Leaders of the Reformation*, ed. R. de Molen, 1985

There is no modern biography of Laud: the best are still:
H. Trevor-Roper, *Archbishop Laud*, 1940
W. Hunt, *The Puritan Movement*, 1982
K. Sharpe, 'Archbishop Laud' *History Today*, August 1983
K. Sharpe, 'Archbishop Laud and the University of Oxford' in *History and Imagination*, ed. H. Lloyd-Jones *et al*, 1981

For the financial and administrative problems of the 1630s, see E. Cope, H. Tomlinson and C. Russell (above). See also:
J. Morrill, *The Revolt of the Provinces*, 2nd edn 1980
K. Sharpe, 'Crown, Parliament and Localities', *English Historical Review*, 1986
P. Lake, 'The Collection of Ship Money in Cheshire', *Northern History*, vol. XVII, 1981

Period 1640–42

It is essential to read Chapter 6 *after* gaining a sense of the course of events as in any of the general surveys or biographies, or the following:
A. Fletcher, *The Outbreak of the English Civil War*, 1979
P. Zagorin, *The Court and the Country*, 1972

The following are also especially useful:
C. Hibbard, *Charles I and the Popish Plot*, 1983
B. Manning, *The English People and the English Revolution*, 1976, esp. Chapters 7 and 8
J. Morrill, 'The Religious Context of the English Civil War', *Transactions of the Royal Historical Society*, 1983
J. Morrill, 'The Attack on the Church of England in the Long Parliament', in *History, Society and the Churches*, eds. D. Beales and G. Best, 1984

Titles in the series:

British Politics in the 1930s and 1940s	Paul Adelman
Change and Continuity in British Society 1800–1850	Richard Brown
Elizabeth I	Geoffrey Regan
Charles I	Christopher W. Daniels and John Morrill

Index